**Praise for Rich
Disney 1
You Can l**

"Your book is a veritable Disney BIBLE! You've told the well-known stories, but added the creative thinking, smart planning, and constant "change" to make it all work. Walt was a dear, dear friend of mine and our families were close."
　　　　　—Art Linkletter, radio-television personality and author,
　　　　　　Old Age is Not for Sissies and *Kids Say the Darndest Things*

"Loaded with information and easy to read! Rich Hamilton has combined stories about Walt Disney with useful success methods that Disney used to create Disneyland. If you like Disneyland, or have ever wondered how Walt Disney came up with the idea and successfully put the business together, read this book."
　　　　　　　　　　　　　　　　　　—Jim Cathcart, author,
　　　　　　　　　The Eight Competencies of Relationship Selling

"Rich Hamilton dissects the magic of Disney in a fun, interesting and user-friendly way. "Disney Magic" clearly is a book of business savvy you can adapt to use personally and professionally."
　　　　　　　—Larry James, CelebrateLove.com, author,
　　　　　　　　　　How to Really Love the One You're With

"Rich Hamilton captures the essential quality of Disney's genius. You're given a rare opportunity of stepping inside the mind of a visionary by exploring the dimensions of Walt Disney's dreams. This book is a "must read" for anyone seriously striving to obtain personal or professional success."
　　　— Carole Copeland Thomas, radio personality, author,
　　　　　　　　　　　　　　　　　　　Personal Empowerment

"Rich Hamilton helps with more than selling and marketing, he knows how to deliver on a dream, plan complex projects, and put together a responsive workforce. Listen carefully to what Rich says about engineering a successful business."
　　　　　　　　　　—Bill Brooks, author, *High Impact Selling*

"Rich Hamilton insists that we can all succeed by applying a few simple methods. Rich's down-to-earth way of looking at business is refreshing. Hamilton is at his best when discussing such specifics as how to give people what they want, how to understand promotion, and how to generate follow-up business."
　　　　—James Malinchak, author, *From College to the Real World*

Books by Rich Hamilton:

*Disney Magic: Business Strategy
You Can Use at Work and at Home*

*Internet Business Magic: Using Disney's
Magic Strategy in Your Own Online Business*

*Disney Magic Ideabook: Using Disney's Magic
Strategy for Your Own Business Success*

Internet Support:

www.MagicStrategy.com

Disney Magic Ideabook
Using Disney's Magic Strategy For Your Own Business Success

"Disneyland is dedicated to the ideals, the dreams, and the hard facts that have created America... with the hope that it will be a source of joy and inspiration to all the world."
—Walt Disney, July 17, 1955

Rich Hamilton

SellBetter Tools
Phoenix, Arizona, USA

Disney Magic Ideabook

First Edition
Copyright © 2004 Rich Hamilton. All Rights Reserved.

ISBN 0-9728476-2-6
Library of Congress Control Number: 2003097371

Publisher's Cataloging-in-Publication Data
(Prepared By Cassidy Cataloguing Services, Inc.)
Hamilton, Rich.

    Disney magic ideabook : using Disney's magic strategy for your own business success / Rich Hamilton. — 1st ed. — Phoenix, Ariz. : SellBetter Tools, 2004.

        p. ; cm.

    Includes bibliographical references and index.
    ISBN 0-9728476-2-6

    1. Success in business. 2. Management. 3. Business planning. 4. Strategic planning. 5. Walt Disney Company. I. Title

HF5386 .H362 2004   2003097371
650.1—dc22   CIP

Walt Disney Company Trademarks: *Disney Magic Ideabook* is not authorized by, endorsed by, or affiliated with The Walt Disney Company, Inc., or any of its theme parks or subsidiaries. Disneyland and The Magic Kingdom are registered trademarks of The Walt Disney Company. Other Disney trademarks include Mickey Mouse, The Mickey Mouse Club, Adventureland, Fantasyland, Tomorrowland, Frontierland, New Orleans Square, Space Mountain, Splash Mountain, Walt Disney World, Disneyland Paris, Epcot Center, Tokyo Disneyland, California Adventure, FastPass and Walt Disney. All references to these and other Disney trademarked properties are used in accordance with the Fair Use Doctrine and are not meant to imply that this book is a Disney product for advertising or other commercial purposes.

Disclaimer: While every precaution has been taken in the preparation of this book, the publisher and author assume no responsibility for errors or omissions. Neither is any liability assumed for damages resulting, or alleged to result, directly or indirectly from the use of the information contained herein. If you do not wish to be bound by the above, you may return this book with receipt to the publisher for a full refund of the purchase price.

Schools and Corporations: This book is available at quantity discounts with bulk purchases for educational or business use. For more information please contact the publisher at the address below.

SellBetter Tools
Box 50186, Phoenix, AZ 85076 • 1-888-240-4742

Manufactured in the United States of America

Acknowledgments

I've been influenced and taught by many talented people over the years, and this book is the result of some powerful collaboration. I'll name just a few.

A personal friend of Walt Disney, Art Linkletter saw my first book, *Disney Magic,* and responded with powerful words of encouragement. I visited with Art just two days before his ninety-first birthday. He told me that in addition to working on a new book, he still skis and surfs. And he encouraged me to do the same for at least another forty years.

Thanks to Bill Johnson, Rick Hubbard, Ken and Skip Pollock, Andrea Ellis, Richard Davis, George Peintner, Ron Dressler, Tony Vicich, and Kevin Dieball. All have encouraged and helped me in my endeavors.

And to Rod Rademacher, Rob McKnight, Fred Conger, Dick Fraley, Bob Freeman, Boyd Rodman, Joe and Marcy Cummins, Keith Lee, Deena Iannella, and Veronica Bahn, thanks for helping me understand certain unique aspects of promotion and marketing.

Special thanks go to the thousands of cast members at Disneyland and Walt Disney World who make the magic every day, and to the hundreds of those cast members who demonstrated and explained to me what they do and how they learn to do it.

To my parents, Martha and Dick Hamilton, who instilled into me a foundation of love, integrity, and curiosity.

To my wife, Sharon, for her confidence in me, for reading and editing my manuscript, and for suffering through the many trips to Disney theme parks for "just another look" to be sure everything was right.

Dedication

*To Walt Disney,
who wanted to make people happy
and in doing that,
gave us this powerful business model.*

Contents

Preface	11
Let us entertain you	14
Disney's unique working atmosphere	16
What do they really do at a Disney theme park?	20
If only I can make you smile	22
Dogs & cats ride the tram at Disneyland	24
Little plastic cards all over the 'world'	25
The most popular passport in the land	26
2 days, 3 days, 4 days or 5?	27
A whole year of magic	28
And more, and more, and more	30
Bring 'em back again and again	33
Make money more fun	35
Give it away or sell it at cost	37
Now you see it, now you don't	38
It's more fun than reading a map	39
The 'Power of Story'	41
Make waiting fun	43
The real solution for long waits	45
The significance of an overflowing trash can	47
Prepare for 'situations'	49
Seeking a Fantasyland trash can pin	50
Cooking with Mickey	53
And the beat goes on…	55
Outrageous hats and mouse ears	57
So many kiosks	58
A special treat from guest relations	60
It's a party in Town Square!	61
Unexpected magic	62
The show after the show	63
An afterthought that made it all work	64
Who are Disney's best customers?	65

After your theme park adventure,
   shop and have dinner 66
Promotion, free advertising, and paid advertising 67
An online money-making machine 69
For a second chance, eBay 71
Partners make a bigger enterprise 72
Sponsorship allows other firms to
   participate in your business 74
Disneyland's secret club 77
Fill your business with people who 'get it' 79
Now, go to Disneyland or Walt Disney World 83
Suggested Reading 85
Index 86

Preface

I laughed when I first saw the drawing on the cover of this book. That's me at Disneyland, sleuthing around looking for the big and small ideas that make Disneyland work magic for guests and staff alike.

Like me, it seems that everyone who visits Disneyland or Walt Disney World takes a lot of pictures. Cameras are everywhere.

As I was writing this book, I visited Disneyland on the occasion of their 48th anniversary. I realized that the pictures I take are different than most folks. While others are snapping photos of their family in front of the castle, I'm taking pictures of trash cans, detailed cracks in the walkway, and menu signs.

While walking through Disney's California Adventure, I was taking a picture of the Coca-Cola sign at the Fill Your Jets refreshment stand. As I lowered my camera, I realized a man at my left was taking a picture of the refreshment stand, too.

Was this a case of "follow-me," someone taking a picture because they saw me taking a picture?

I watched a bit longer, and he moved around and took another picture of the refreshment stand. I became even more curious. "Who is this guy who takes pictures of the same things I take pictures of?" I wondered.

Then I noticed he was wearing a Disney name badge.

I looked back at the refreshment stand, and realized he wasn't photographing the stand, or the sign, as I was. He was photographing the Disney employee – they call them cast members – who was working there.

This young woman was standing, leaning back against the stand. Her arms were crossed, and her face was frowning. She looked so unhappy to be there, I suspected she had come to work with a hangover. This did not project the Disney image at all, and, as I probably don't need to tell you, no one was buying any soft drinks from her.

I quickly decided to watch the Disney man with the camera, who I suddenly suspected to be a manager. Like any good sleuth, I followed him.

As he walked back toward the center of the park, he slipped his digital camera into his pocket and pulled a cell phone out of the other pocket, placing a call. Suddenly he stopped, turned around, and headed a different direction. I surmised that he had found the woman's direct supervisor was not where he expected.

Now he walked toward the back of the park, in front of the winery. He leaned over and picked up a piece of trash in the middle of the walkway, then quickly deposited it in a trash can and continued walking. I followed until he disappeared into a "cast member only" door which led to backstage offices.

Several things were illustrated here, some through the manager's actions and some by general observation.

First, the cast member's "sour" expression and her "unhappy" posture were in stark contrast to what we see with most cast members. As an *example by exception,* it's clear Disney expects and usually gets better behavior from their cast. Indeed, a few minutes after witnessing this sequence of events, I walked over to Disneyland and shared the story with a security screener (a very "happy" security screener, I might add). She was visibly shocked by what I said. "Gosh, that's unusual," she said. "You won't find me like that. See my smile?" she laughed.

With the camera, the manager documented the situation, and immediately sought the woman's direct supervisor. The supervisor could then take corrective measures.

Along the way, the manager picked up trash and disposed of it. I've heard for years that at every level, managers will stop and pick up trash. Even the presidents of Disneyland and Walt Disney World, Matt Ouimet and Al Weiss, will pick up trash, because it sets the proper example for all cast members. So they all pick up trash, and the parks, even backstage, stay clean.

But because it works so well, and the parks stay so clean, this is the first time I actually witnessed a manager picking up trash.

It's an example of Disney's "manage by example" philosophy. It's better than managing by objectives or results, and worlds ahead of "managing by walking around." Further, Disney proves that it works.

Today and every day your customers and your associates compare you with the best run companies in the universe. One of those is

Disney, and the Disney experience is remarkable at the theme parks where the customer experience is superb and the employee satisfaction is high.

In my book, *Disney Magic: Business Strategy You Can Use at Work and at Home,* I explored the Disney theme park business and organized the business in a progressive, strategic manner. In the process, I discovered a number of good ideas that didn't quite fit in that volume.

It's those ideas you'll find here, organized as a collection of essays. Some I wrote about in the other book, some are fully unique here.

Some of the ideas you read here will not seem new or earth-shattering, because they make sense.

That's what you want, isn't it? *Ideas that make sense?*

And you may be doing many of these things already. Frankly, I hope so.

I expect you will find some new ideas as well, and awaken a few ideas that you've thought about but not put into action.

In addition, I want to give you special gifts, including a set of "mini-posters" that will remind you of certain principles revealed in this book, and a subscription to our online *Magic Strategy* newsletter, designed to help you implement the ideas discovered at Disney theme parks. To get these gifts, go now to our website:

www.MagicStrategy.com

To access the special gift section for readers of this book click on the "Members" button. Your special access code is 1928. (That's the year Mickey Mouse was introduced.)

Walt Disney, and the Walt Disney Company, have created success with the theme park business by putting together a combination of good ideas and good execution. They not only have good ideas, they execute them well.

It's my hope that as you read this book you will discover a set of linked ideas that you will apply to your life and your business. I hope you'll recognize the material that's good for you, and that you're able to execute the ideas well.

Let us entertain you

"When you're onstage, everything matters," one woman, a former Disneyland cast member, was telling me. "No slouching, and no leaning, that was the number one rule. Everything had to look good, look friendly. We had to be friendly. And it was a good thing."

"I talk with a lot of cast members when I visit," I told her. "And a lot of people wonder how I'm able to get them to talk to me."

"That's easy," she said. "We are supposed to engage guests in conversation when we can. If you have a question, we're supposed to answer it. And if we can do something to get you to smile, that's the goal. So sure, it's easy to get cast members to answer your questions."

It wasn't too hard for the folks at Disneyland to think of themselves as entertainers. After all, the parent company was the Disney studios, and they were turning out live action features, cartoons, and feature animation films.

So, when you go to Disneyland or Walt Disney World, you'll find that their employees, who they call "cast members," think of themselves as entertainers and when they are in front of their customers ("guests"), they consider themselves to be "onstage."

It's all part of a rather involved culture that Disney has developed over time to establish a unique perspective on customer service.

Here's the point:

I don't care whether you're in products or services, selling hamburgers, cars, or computer consulting. You're in the entertainment business.

In fact, every business is in the entertainment business.

The doctor's office is in the entertainment business. Sure, the medical care needs to be good, but the doctor that gets repeat business from cooperative patients is the one with the "bedside manner," the staff that smiles and makes patients feel better, and the waiting room that's fun rather than intimidating.

Selling advertising? You'll do best if you entertain your customer.

That does *not* mean you should take them to lunch and dinner, or treat them to professional baseball tickets, although that *might* be part of the mix.

And it does *not* mean you need to tell jokes all day.

Entertaining your customer simple means they should have a good time doing business with you.

Walt Disney said he wanted guests to walk away from Disneyland with smiles on their faces.

And that's the key to making *any* business attractive to customers.

Most people go to Disneyland or Walt Disney World to "ride the rides" and have a good time.

At a Disney theme park, a lot more goes into giving you a "good time" than fun attractions.

It starts with attractive landscaping, a "storybook" appearance, and a Mickey Mouse face created with flowers at the entry.

Then you'll find live music. Maybe the Disneyland Band, or a barbershop quartet on Main Street.

Everything will be neat and clean.

And the Disney employees will be friendly.

You'll hear a funny "honk" from an old car on Main Street.

And you'll smell a tasty aroma coming from the candy store.

It creates a fun atmosphere that makes it fun both for guests and for Disney cast members.

In a different way, you can make the experience of doing business with your firm pleasant for your customers and fellow employees.

Make your business fun, interesting, and exciting!

Disney's unique working atmosphere

A spunky Mickey Mouse appeared over 75 years ago, but it didn't take long before Walt Disney realized Mickey's character needed to "shape up" a bit and begin to watch his behavior.

Walt knew he needed to appeal to an audience across the entire country, and because Walt was reared in Missouri, he had a clear understanding of Midwestern values.

Some time before Disneyland was completed in 1955, Walt recognized that the name "Disney" meant more than him and his creations. The name had taken on a life of its own, representing good, wholesome fun. Disney movies were expected to reflect that wholesomeness, and Disneyland had to reflect it as well.

Walt also knew that he wanted certain things to happen in Disneyland, based on his negative experiences in most other amusement parks to that time.

Three values were considered most desirable:
1. Most amusement parks were disorganized combinations of rather plain rides. Walt wanted Disneyland to give guests a good show.
2. Most were unclean, sometimes filthy properties. Walt wanted Disneyland to be spotlessly clean.
3. The people who worked at most amusement parks were often unfriendly and sometimes a scary, unsavory lot. Walt wanted Disneyland to be staffed by clean, friendly people.

It is remarkable that Disney was able to accomplish that when he built Disneyland.

It's even more remarkable that today, over 35 years after Walt's death, customer surveys show that the three things guests report as most impressive at Disneyland and Walt Disney World are: (1) the good show, (2) the place is clean, and (3) the people are friendly. Those are the very values Walt regarded as so important.

A lot of things have gone into making that happen.

Walt recognized that the company would be hiring a lot of new people. And he wanted to be sure those people understood what was supposed to happen. I described this in detail in *Disney Magic,* but here are the key ideas.

One of the most important was the creation of Disney University in 1955. It's more of a training process than an institution. It's used to provide orientation training to new employees and continuing leadership training to all employees.

Traditions. It starts with values like honesty, reliability, loyalty, and respect for people as individuals. Belief in innovation and a common focus are important at Disney. From values come the history and philosophy that make Disney theme parks what they are.

A special language. They look at Disneyland as a large outdoor show, where everyone has an important role.

Disney has no customers. They play *host* to *guests.* A crowd is an *audience.*

The employees are *cast members.* Cast members work *onstage* or *backstage.* Uniforms are *costumes.* Instead of rides, they have *attractions* or *adventures.*

Today they would call Disneyland (or the parks at Walt Disney World) a *theme park,* but in the early days of Disneyland it was an *environmental park,* or, just *Disneyland.* There wasn't anything else like it.

A first name policy. Walt said, "Call me Walt. The only 'Mr.' we have around here is Mr. Toad." Soon after Disneyland opened, the cast members were given name tags with their first name on them.

The Disneyland Look. Disney knew costumes would play an important role in creating the image he wanted. They had to be designed right, kept clean and in good repair.

Beyond costumes, the cast members needed to project that clean, wholesome look that we think of as Disney. Neat, well-groomed cast members enhance the image. Walt didn't want the fantasy of Disneyland ruined by the encroachment of modern society and contemporary fashion and grooming.

Hair must be neat and trimmed. Jewelry is limited. Visible tattoos and body piercings are restricted.

The "Disney Look" has changed occasionally through the years. For some time no facial hair was allowed, but now men may sport conservative moustaches if they wish.

All this is made clear when cast members are hired, so there's seldom any problem later.

The application to your business?

Consider the values of your company.

Write up your company's history and traditions, so you have an understanding of what makes the company what it is today.

We've already discussed how everyone is in the entertainment business. Disney used show business terms to create a language that changed how everyone approached their roles (jobs).

Certain parts of the show business terminology might apply to your business. Certainly, the guest-host terminology fits nearly any organization.

I've always thought it admirable when a government agency or a corporate support department starts thinking of doing transactions with "customers," but trying to install a customer relationship in the internal business transaction is really a misguided effort. That's because most people don't look at the customer relationship with enough understanding.

Instead, the guest-host terminology sets up better expectations.

Walt Disney thought that while many people didn't know how to take care of a customer very well, most knew how to be a good host to a guest. I'm not sure that's as true today as it was in 1955, but it still sets up an expectation of a certain graciousness and helpful interaction.

The first name policy within the company helps create more personal relationships, engendering better cooperation. The name tags, even in a small firm, will help customers deal with people on a first-name basis. And in a larger firm, it puts people at ease when they encounter someone they don't know, or know only incidentally.

Finally, the Disneyland look creates an image reflecting the values and traditions of the company. While many resist a uniform, guidelines or a "dress code" will provide customers and fellow employees with an atmosphere that says something about the company.

Personal grooming says a lot about the individual, but reflects on the company at the same time.

While Disney's approach may seem extreme, a look at other companies suggests its power. For example, IBM became the leader in the computer field with pinstripe suits and white dress shirts. Their competitors who deviated from that power suit came in behind them. While some will debate how much was related to clothing and grooming, experts in the field have tested the suit and proven its effect.

What do they really do at a Disney theme park?

Once the culture is identified, defined, and used in training, it needs to be translated into operating terms.

That starts with the service theme. At Disney, it's "We create happiness by providing quality entertainment for people of all ages, everywhere."

When Walt Disney expressed it, he said, "My business is making people, especially children, happy." While Walt may have kept children in mind, he also wanted to entertain adults; that was one of the goals in building the park.

As Disneyland opened, the training described it very simply, "We create happiness."

I think it's interesting that he defined the business in terms of his customers' or guests' emotions. He didn't define the business in terms of films, or cartoons, or toys, or even an amusement park. He didn't string together a list of seemingly unrelated businesses. Walt wanted to create happiness.

What emotion does your organization want to deliver?

Disney's service theme suggests a formula that might help you create a service theme:

> We create (*what emotion?*)
> By providing (*what products or services?*)
> For (*who?*) (*where?*)

Core Purpose

Within the service theme, you can create a "purpose statement" that clarifies the core purpose for your staff.

Lee Cockerell, Executive Vice President of Walt Disney World Operations, says every cast member has the same purpose, "To give our guests the best vacation they've ever had."

That applies, he says, to everyone. Dishwashers know they will ruin that experience if a guest is served with a dirty glass or silverware. Housekeepers know the guest's going to be disappointed if there are crumbs in the bedding.

Cockerell tells of a parade manager who thought her job was managing the parade. When she began thinking of making guests happy, she had new drive to get the parade out on time, to have everyone in place, and to have the music properly synchronized.

Service standards

Once you've decided on your Service Theme and Core Purpose, you can move on to Service Standards. Disney's service standards are Safety, Courtesy, Show, and Efficiency.

Within each of these four areas, Disney establishes definitions and standards for the park and for each attraction.

Finally, Delivery Systems are established. These are:

Cast. The employees create and deliver the entertainment, so attention is given to the process of how they function so that this continues positively over time. Hiring, training, rehearsing, and taking care of the employees is covered in more detail in *Disney Magic*.

Setting. The setting is defined as "onstage," or anywhere that there is customer contact, and it's a delivery system because it's part of the show. In other companies, it might include work or production areas that do not involve customer contact, if it's part of the deliverable.

Operating systems. All the behind-the-scenes systems that keep the organization running are included here. Think of scheduling, production, purchasing and receiving, billing, banking and utilities.

When it's all operating correctly, the systems work together smoothly and guests don't even realize what's happening.

If only I can make you smile

The first day on the job, Disney begins teaching cast members that it's important to create "magic moments" for the guests.

A magic moment is an interaction with the guest that results in a smile.

A guest in a Disney theme park for a day probably has the opportunity to interact with a cast member 100 times or so. Disney reasons that if each of those interactions could bring a smile to the face of the guest, the overall experience will be good.

For example, a cast member who is loading guests on a ride like the Matterhorn could be saying, "Watch your step… watch your step… watch your step…" The job would be pretty monotonous and the guests would simply be loaded.

But if the cast member can see each guest as an individual, and notice what they're wearing, carrying, or saying, the job gets more interesting and guests can enjoy a personal magic moment.

Imagine this, "Oh, I like your shirt, watch your step… Neat backpack, watch your step… Cute shoes, watch your step… Where did you find those cool jeans? Really? Watch your step… I see your Aladdin shirt, have you seen the show at Disney's California Adventure? Watch your step…"

It's harder work, requires thinking and multi-tasking, but adds interest to the day and delights the guests.

Most magic moments are short, one to three second interactions like these.

Others may be more involved, like when a cast member in a store picks up the phone and tries to track down the Cinderella costume you want for your granddaughter.

Or when you ask about the balcony at the Disney Gallery and a cast member tells you the history of the facility, and you picture Walt Disney and his brother Roy sitting out there having breakfast, watching the fully loaded Mark Twain steam by on the Rivers of America.

In addition, park management tries to develop attractions and events which will bring smiles to guests' faces. These "organized" magic moments include certain features in parades, live entertainment, and the design of rides and facilities.

Magic moments are probably the most powerful tool in the Disney arsenal. Because Disney focuses on providing many of these events each day for every guest, and because they have named them "magic moments," they become real and manageable.

Disney expects to create magic moments for cast members, too, and for the cast to create them for each other. The idea is that it takes a happy cast to provide a happy guest experience.

Every business can benefit from the concept of creating many magic moments for their employees and customers every day. Think about things you might do, and the things others could do, when you're on the job.

Dogs & cats ride the tram at Disneyland

On our way to Disneyland, we picked up our adult son in San Diego, where he was on temporary assignment with the US Coast Guard. I should say we picked up our son *and his dog*.

Like many people who travel, the dog is a constant companion. At times this can be challenging.

At Disneyland it's easy.

The dog rode the tram with us to the entrance area. We made our way over to the kennel, and left the dog there for the day. The small fee seemed reasonable, and we could go back any time to exercise her.

I even enjoy joking about how much the dog enjoyed riding on the tram. (As my son will confirm, she *really did* seem to enjoy it.)

Should you offer kennel services? Probably not, but *maybe*.

The point is to make it easy for people to do business with you.

Without the kennel, it would be much harder for a lot of people to visit Disneyland. Most of them would simply do something else for the day.

Make it easy to buy. Provide extra customer services.

A gym near my house offers free 24-hour childcare, so parents can exercise any time they want without worrying about their children.

The Disneyland Kennel opened in 1958. The business model is interesting:

1. It attracts guests who might not come otherwise.
2. The small fee covers much of the cost.
3. When we went it was sponsored by Friskies, so Friskies got the advertising value and Disney netted the sponsorship revenue.

Little plastic cards all over the 'world'

When I first visited Walt Disney World in 1986, they had a sponsorship agreement with MasterCard, and you couldn't use your Visa card in the park.

Imagine how many people this upset after they spent their money getting there and suddenly found they were "broke," because they couldn't use their credit cards? Lots of unhappy guests.

Imagine how much this cost Disney when guests had to get by on the cash in their pockets!

They figured it out and now Disney takes *all* major credit cards.

Do you? If not, rethink this policy.

For years American Express was a sponsor at Disneyland, and their cards were the "official card of Disneyland." Visa now has that sponsorship distinction but the point is this: Whoever is the official card, Disney honors all cards.

Why? Because their customers want to use them.

Now look at your business.

A major electronics store not far from my home refuses to take American Express. I wrote the company to suggest that they take the card and they replied, "it costs too much to take American Express."

Discounters like WalMart and Kmart take American Express. Other electronics stores take the card. So do office supply stores and a number of other competitors. American Express cardholders just go somewhere else.

A small business near me refuses to take one card, because they made the owner mad once several years ago. I have no idea what the story is, but he thinks he's hurting the card company. Actually, he's chosen to penalize his customers.

And that costs *him* business.

The most popular passport in the land

When Disneyland opened, Disney followed the traditional amusement park pricing with an admission required to get in the park and additional tickets required for each ride. The general admission was one dollar. Ride tickets were ten to thirty-five cents each.

Within a few months, tickets were sold in a "book" with an admission ticket and an assortment of ride tickets for a bundled price. As the day went on, you would buy additional ride tickets for the rides you most wanted to ride, or you could buy an additional book of tickets.

In 1982, Disney eliminated the individual ride tickets and started issuing "passports" for twelve dollars each. A passport covers admission plus all the main rides and attractions.

By 2003 the price reached $47 at Disneyland.

There were several advantages to this approach.

No longer would anyone complain about unused tickets left in a ticket book. They eliminated the expense of printing, selling, and collecting tickets. Everybody got the "full experience," meaning that every guest enjoyed rides all day long without having to buy additional tickets.

Guests would come and stay longer, since the higher price included so much.

How can you apply this in your business? Or, if you're already bundling products and services, are there more creative ways you can bundle or package things so customers buy more?

2 days, 3 days, 4 days or 5?

Another offering at Disney theme parks is the "Multi-Day Passport." This is an admission ticket that admits a person for several days, generally at a discounted price. The guest gets a discount, and Disney gets a "promise" to return again and again.

As I write this, Disneyland is promoting a five-day park-hopper passport, good for five days in the parks. It has to be bought online or through an advance vacation package; you can't buy it at the main gate ticket office. The five days may be used any time before the end of the year. And the cost is about the same as three single day admissions.

On a recent trip to Disneyland I met a family from Mexico. They were finishing up their fifth day at the Disneyland Resort, and the next day they were going to Magic Mountain. The morning after that would mark their return home to Mexico.

Because Disney offered a five-day passport, they spent *most* of their week-long vacation at the Disney properties. The competition got only one day.

You can do about the same thing, bundling your offering into a multiple item, multiple day, or repeat package.

A whole year of magic

"Let's run over to Disneyland tonight for dinner," I told my wife. And we did exactly that. Had dinner, rode one or two rides, and went back to the hotel.

It was 1992. I found we were going to California six or eight times a year, usually staying in or near Anaheim. I almost always found an excuse to spend a day at Disneyland. But it was too expensive to pay admission just to go for dinner.

Then I discovered the "annual passport."

When I first bought an annual passport, I was delighted with the freedom it afforded. I could arrive in Anaheim late in the day and still venture into the park, at a time when buying a full day passport wouldn't make sense. Sometimes before leaving town, we would go to Disneyland for breakfast, and leave at mid-morning.

Disney sells a "Premium Annual Passport" which includes regular admission to Disneyland and Disney's California Adventure parks for a full year. Free parking is also included, along with a limited discount program that provides discounts on certain shopping and restaurant purchases.

As of 2003, they sell that pass for $225, just a little less than 5 regular days admission (at $47 each). Anyone who expects to visit Disneyland five or more days in the coming year is well advised to buy the premium passport.

Running over to Disneyland for dinner wouldn't have been practical if I'd been buying regular admission tickets.

Disney offers a less expensive annual passport for $165. It has about 35 "blackout days" when it can't be used, including most Saturdays and holidays. You forego the parking and discounts. But it provides extensive access at a lower price.

So the annual passport is a good deal for guests. And there's a similar offering at Walt Disney World.

What does it do for Disney?

It rewards Disney's most loyal customers, and gives them added incentive to return again and again. After all, since I've already paid my admission, why would I want to go to a competitive park where I'd have to ante up the entrance fee?

In the process, I'll likely bring along friends who pay.

And I'll buy more food and more merchandise.

My "contract" with Disney gets me admission for the whole year. Their "contract" with me buys my loyalty.

This concept can apply to nearly any company where there is an opportunity for repeat business.

Think of the bookstores that have annual memberships that entitle members to special discounts on all the books they buy.

Some theatres have memberships that result in reduced admission prices, preview shows, and special arts series.

How about the car wash that offers an annual plan for all the car washes you want for a year? Same idea.

I belong to an association that charges annual dues plus a monthly meeting fee. I suggested a full year option, including annual dues and monthly fees, at a discount. The association gets the money early and the member gets a discount. And with the full year option it "costs" the member for *not* attending, instead of the other way around.

And more, and more, and more

You bought your admission to Disneyland, and it includes admission to the attractions inside. You're done spending money, right? Wrong!

In 1982, when Disney combined attractions with the admission fee, offering "passports," they enhanced the experience in many ways. But they know that for every 50-dollar admission, they will still realize another fifty or more in additional sales. Average.

Characters

Early in Walt Disney's career he discovered that he could add income by licensing his cartoon characters for dolls, shirts, watches, juices, tablets, and more.

In the park, the Disney characters are merchandised heavily. Store after store sells all kinds of products with Disney characters on them.

Plush toys are favorites, but they also sell t-shirts, sweatshirts, watches, costumes, pencils, pens, erasers, backpacks, purses, notepads, pins, even cell phone holsters.

Thousands of autograph books and pens are sold every week, and eager youngsters run, then stand in line to meet a character and get an autograph. (The actors who play the parts are trained to sign the character's autographs alike. And unlike the "real world," they seek the character's signature... not the actor's.)

Attraction products

Disney moves beyond the characters and creates products for the attractions, so you'll find a sweatshirt for Pirates of the Caribbean and a watch for Space Mountain,

In the specialty parks you'll find specialty merchandise, like a *Home Improvement* "Tool Time" t-shirt in the MGM-Disney Studios.

Of course, they make products for the parks in general, including Disneyland sweatshirts, Epcot t-shirts, and Animal Kingdom polo shirts.

And they sell a constantly changing array of postcards, books, and other souvenirs.

Just being there

The very fact that you're onsite leads to a wide variety of additional products and services that Disney is only too happy to provide.

At refreshment kiosks, in fast service and full service restaurants they provide an array of different breakfasts, lunches, and dinners. Kiosks scattered around the property sell bottled water, soft drinks, popcorn, and other treats.

Families rent strollers, the disabled rent wheelchairs, and groups rent walkie-talkies.

Kodak estimates that four percent of all amateur photographs taken in the United States are taken at Disneyland or Walt Disney World. So Disney sells film and cameras.

Continuously Plussing

Stores and kiosks are located throughout the theme parks, but there's a reason Main Street USA is at the front of the Magic Kingdom. It's mostly stores and restaurants, so you begin your visit with a strong merchandising effort, and you end it with another walk through the Disney "shopping mall."

I've even heard parents telling their children, "Just relax. We'll go through the stores on the way out so we don't have to carry what you buy all day."

And Disney plans for that, normally keeping Main Street USA open an hour after the rest of the park closes.

At Disney theme parks, you will continuously find reasons to part with more money.

It's good business.

After all, that's why grocery stores went self-service in the middle of the last century. As did most other stores.

And why all that merchandise is loaded on displays around the cash register. It's a "point of purchase" enticement.

Do you do that in your business? Think about add-on sales you might make to plus your business.

Photographers add albums and frames. Some add-on makeup and skin care products.

Bookstores add-on bookmarks, cards, and top sellers.

When you place an order on the telephone, you're often offered an additional special "sale" item, or a price incentive to increase your order.

Disney demonstrates one of the most important marketing strategies we've found: It's cheaper to sell more to an existing customer than it is to find a new customer.

And the easiest time to make that sale is while they're already buying.

Bring 'em back again and again

"We have to bring the kids back to see this," my wife said, after seeing *Disney's Aladdin—A Musical Spectacular* at Disney's California Adventure shortly after the Broadway-style production premiered. "In fact," she continued, "Brian will want to see this. And Susan. And our next-door neighbors."

Keep in mind that we live in another state, so this isn't just a trip across town to the amusement park.

When Walt Disney located Disneyland in Anaheim, many thought he was crazy, putting it out in the middle of an unpopulated agricultural area. But he did it following research that indicated it would be quite near the geographic center of population in coming years.

The research has proven accurate, and now, some 50 years later, there's little agricultural use left in the area. (Maybe *none*, since Disney bought the strawberry fields southeast of Disneyland for a future park development.)

The result is that Disneyland enjoys a high percentage of return visitors, people from Southern California who return many times each year. Some come back every week.

Walt Disney World enjoys a large number of visitors who return once or twice a year from throughout the eastern US.

Walt instinctively knew from the beginning that he wanted people to return again and again.

That's why he planned on exquisite details in park design, so people would see something new each time they came. And he said, "Disneyland will never be finished." By continuing to develop new attractions, he would be giving people new reasons to return.

This is an extension of the marketing strategy, "It's cheaper to sell more to an existing customer than it is to find a new customer."

Studies I've seen say it costs five to ten times more to bring in a new customer than it does to bring a previous customer back.

Of course, that only works if you've given them a good experience in the first place, and if there's a reason to come back. Some businesses lend themselves to continued business.

Disney does it with multi-day passports, annual passes, and by promoting new attractions and special events, holidays, and celebrations.

A dental practice suggests six-month cleanings and checkups, and sets the appointment before you leave.

The family photographer suggests an annual holiday portrait, and mails special offers to previous customers.

An auto service facility has a discount coupon for your *next* oil change, and gives one to *every customer.*

It only works if you realize what you have to offer and promote your customers' return. How can you promote return customers?

Comeback coupons, multi-date packaging, and service contracts all create a stronger relationship.

In fact, "relationship" may define the real secret.

What can you do to build a stronger relationship with your customer so they want to come back?

Make money more fun

When you buy your ticket to Disneyland or Walt Disney World, you may be asked if you want to buy some "Disney Dollars."

Disney Dollars are certificates that look something like currency, but they have Mickey Mouse and other characters on them instead of presidents, and they're printed in full color. They're usable as cash anywhere in a Disney resort (or the Disney Stores), and when you leave you can turn them back for regular currency. Or, since they don't expire, you can use them on a later visit.

If you're buying your admission with a credit card, you can also buy Disney Dollars, giving you extra "cash" to spend in the park at refreshment stands, restaurants, and stores.

With the clever designs and Disney characters, they even become collectors items, and Disney comes out with new designs regularly to encourage this.

Disney Dollars do several things for Disney.

On one hand, they're like gift certificates, but they're in currency denominations so they handle them like cash, without the normal paperwork of a gift certificate.

If you buy them and keep them awhile, Disney gets the use of your money. (And if you lose them, frame them, or put them away as a souvenir, Disney gets to *keep* the money.)

When some are kept as collectors items, it's as if someone paid a dollar, five dollars, or ten dollars for a piece of paper.

When you bought them on your credit card, you may not have the same attachment to them as you do with "real" dollars, and you may spend them more freely.

And even though you can turn them in for cash as you leave, you may have an inclination to go ahead and spend them instead.

Some people will buy them and give them as gifts. Those may or may not all get spent with Disney.

Most businesses wouldn't have the opportunity to design and print collectible gift certificates, because you don't have the lovable Disney characters.

But it's an interesting approach to gift certificates.

Think about it. First, it's valuable to have a gift certificate program. Gift certificates buy loyalty and referrals.

The "dollar" certificate approach (rather than calling them "gift" certificates) lends itself to selling them for a guest's own use. If I'm arriving with my family for a weekend, I may buy several hundred dollars in Disney Dollars on my credit card, and spend freely from that during my stay.

The lack of expiration date and the policy of freely converting them to cash avoids most legal concerns.

Give it away or sell it at cost

It cost 24 cents to print and sell the Disneyland Souvenir Guide in the late 1950's. The company sold it for a quarter, so it was making only a penny. The merchandising department pitched Walt on increasing the price.

"I don't care about making money on this," he answered. What I want is as many of these souvenir guides as possible on people's coffee tables. I want others to see what Disneyland is all about and come for a visit. We'll make our money when they actually come to Disneyland."

Today, that guide sells for about eight dollars, but every guest is offered a free full-color map and schedule when they enter the park. Those maps are often kept as souvenirs (and sell a few years later on eBay for as much as ten bucks).

Walt Disney was savvy about merchandising products, but he wasn't going to let the drive for profit interfere with promoting the park.

What can you do to capitalize on this idea? After all, you don't have the Disneyland name or Mickey Mouse to promote your business. And a sweatshirt that says "Acme Chimney Cleaning" might delight you but most of your customers wouldn't want one.

Think of a product that is desirable, informational, and in the process promotes your business. Give it value. Then give it away or sell it for virtually nothing.

For example, I know a carpet cleaner who wrote a short booklet filled with information about carpets, how to maintain them, how they should be cleaned, and how to find a competent carpet cleaner that does a good job at a reasonable price.

He no longer advertises his carpet cleaning service; he advertises the booklet. People who read the booklet hire him to clean their carpets, because the information is good, and he's the trusted vendor who has achieved "top-of-mind."

Now you see it, now you don't

"I see it," I said to Sharon as we went through Pirates of the Caribbean. "The hidden Mickey on the fort. Do you see it?" I was pointing to the wall of the fort.

"No, I don't see it," was her reply.

I've seen lots of hidden Mickeys at Disneyland, but I'd never found one on the fort, though I'd been told it was there. Of course, once I saw it, it was obvious.

Disney's Imagineers have hidden drawings of Mickey Mouse in strange locations throughout the park. I've found many of them, usually as simple as three circles arranged to depict Mickey. At one point, officials tried to deny their existence. Now they simply say that people find more than were put in place by designers.

The marketing point is this: By creating a "secret" puzzle, repeat visitors have something new to find, at little or no cost to the company.

I looked in Pirates for years before I found that Mickey on the old fort.

It's a great idea: Hide a puzzle in the business.

It might be a good idea to offer a prize for guests who find the answer. In Disney's case, the reward is simple. It's the satisfaction of finding the hidden Mickey.

Disney occasionally releases certain collectible merchandise in limited quantities at various locations around the park. The guest's challenge is to recognize the opportunity and make the purchase.

You might do this with special merchandise, or by offering a special price for a limited time.

When you tantalize your customers with puzzles and secrets, you give them a whole new dimension of entertainment.

It's more fun than reading a map

"We've been coming to Disneyland for years," I told the cast member at the tour desk. "Is there anything, like a backstage tour, that would interest us?"

I fully expected the answer to be no, but was hoping for some kind of behind the scenes adventure.

"We don't do backstage tours anymore at Disneyland," she explained. "But we have a wonderful tour called, 'A Walk with Walt,' that you'll like. It's designed to be the tour Walt would give you if you accompanied him on an early walk around Disneyland, focusing on the design and history of the park."

In one sense, every guest at Disneyland is "on a tour." Every guest, even without a formal tour group, has to plan where to go, what to see next, and when to eat, shop, and leave.

But some guests want, or need, something more. A tour provides a special, personal, more high-touch method of experiencing the resort. *After* paying to get inside Disneyland, the guest pays *again* in order to go on a tour.

Many would say a tour is a joke someplace like Disneyland or Walt Disney World. They would suggest that you can start anywhere, and just make your way around the park.

Others may be overwhelmed, and welcome some guidance, as well as the opportunity to learn more about the design and history of the attractions.

Tours might not seem appropriate to your business, but think of the concept. Some customers need something extra, a guided "tour" of how to enjoy purchasing your products or services.

How daunting is it to buy a computer, wondering if you're buying what you need? Wouldn't a short tour or class on buying a computer be helpful for many people you know? Follow it up with a series of classes on how to use the computer and it's various software packages.

In my software business, I had clients who didn't want to read the manual. Instead, they preferred to pay up to $500 an hour to call me on the phone. I'd read the manual to them. They wanted the personal touch, which included having someone who knew which part of the manual they needed to read.

Craft stores often run classes to teach popular craft projects and art techniques. Music stores offer lessons on various instruments.

It's all another way to serve your customers better, to make them feel special, and to experience your business in a different way.

The 'Power of Story'

"I must be crazy," I thought, as I watched the logs loaded with people careening down the 52-foot flume at Splash Mountain. I was standing in line with my family, and soon I, too, would be crashing into the watery briar patch below.

As Walt Disney matured in the cartoon industry, he moved from cartoons with short "gags" to developing characters and telling more complex stories.

He carried this into Disneyland, so today at the Disney theme parks most attractions tell a story. The story may not always be clear to you as a guest, but as you experience the attraction, the story line provides cohesiveness and allows the adventure to grow, sometimes to a powerful conclusion.

After loading into our Splash Mountain logs, we floated calmly around a corner. Soon we were hauled up the mountain. Along the "river," we saw calm scenes, then floated into a cave. We were looking for our "Laughing Place" as we followed in the footsteps of Brer Rabbit.

In the back of my mind, I knew that giant flume drop into the water of the briar patch was ahead.

Along the way there were several other drops, and the music became more ominous. Finally, our log was pulled up a long track to the top of the mountain. The drop I feared must be coming soon.

Sure enough, we turned a corner and took the plunge, down a long flume into a fog that concealed our path into the briar patch. I closed my eyes, screamed, and splashed into something, I'm not sure what. Moments later we were in the midst of a "Zip-A-Dee-Doo-Dah" celebration. It must be the Laughing Place.

Some attractions, like Great Moments with Mr. Lincoln, use real history. Most use "invented" history. A story is created, and a complete history is developed around that story. Then the ride is designed to incorporate that history and story.

Disney calls it the "Power of Story."

Whether it's Indiana Jones and the Temple of the Forbidden Eye, or the Lion King Celebration parade, the story is what makes the magic in the attraction.

That's why Splash Mountain is so much more popular than the Grizzly River Run at Disney's California Adventure. Grizzly has decorations around a theme, but if it has a story, it's hard to place.

What's *your* story?

Is there a way to weave a story around what you do, and through the facilities you control? It will make it much more interesting.

Make waiting fun

"You mean there's more?" Pat was surprised. Pat and her husband had joined Sharon and me at the Disneyland Resort. We'd entered Jim Henson's Muppet Vision at Disney's California Adventure.

For ten minutes or so we had been in a surreal playland, watching Muppets on multiple television screens carry on about getting ready for a show.

Pat's surprise came when it was time to move on into the full theatre. "I thought *that* was the show!" she told me.

Early in Disneyland's life, Walt discovered that the lines to ride attractions were much too long. He and his staff came up with two ideas to resolve the problem.

First, lines were organized so they went back and forth, instead of one long, extended line. This concept has been adopted by many firms; you find it in restaurants, movie theatres and banks, among others.

The second idea was to create a "pre-show," something in the line or waiting area that would entertain people.

Sometimes it's a matter of decor, with pictures and placards explaining the history of Disney, the subject of the attraction, or building the basic story of the attraction itself.

Soarin' Over California features historical pictures of the aviation industry, in a building designed to look like a big airplane hangar.

The line for Big Thunder Mountain Railroad winds through an old western town and gulch.

While folks are lining up for a parade, Disney sends out vendors with drinks and treats. And they send out entertainers who sing, do magic, and play with the kids seated on the curb.

Some attractions have very elaborate pre-show areas, like Indiana Jones and the Temple of the Forbidden Eye and Star Tours, tied directly to the attraction story.

What about your customers? When they have to wait for service, is it a chore, or do you entertain them?

A waiting area needs to be so much more than a few chairs and a television set. Add a play area for kids. Give people something to do. Offer books for sale or loan. It's okay to sell something, as long as it's not a hard sell.

The real solution for long waits

"I felt guilty walking past those people who were standing in a 45-minute line," Skip told me. Our next door neighbors, she and Ken had met some of their family at Disneyland for a one-day visit in mid-July.

Before they made the trip, we planned the day at Disneyland.

"It was amazing," Ken told me afterward. "We rode all the major rides before noon. My son, Cam, told me that they've spent the whole day and not ridden so many rides. This time the longest line we stood in was 11 minutes."

The secret was arriving early and planning the sequence to use FastPass tickets on the busiest rides.

The FastPass system allows guests to insert their park passport into a FastPass machine, and the machine issues a specific attraction ticket that allows the user to go to a "short line." Those without FastPass tickets have to go to the longer standby line.

The machines will issue a limited number of FastPass tickets for each attraction, and each is stamped with a return time, keeping the short line short.

Every guest has the opportunity to use the FastPass machines. Pick up a FastPass for Indiana Jones, and while you wait for your time window you can take in another attraction, eat lunch, or do some shopping.

It hasn't always been this way.

"I just can't stand in another long line," I remember telling my wife, Sharon. We were thinking about making another trip to Disneyland. And we remembered the long lines on a busy, hot July afternoon.

We did go back, and over time we figured out which attractions to ride early to avoid the longer lines of the afternoon. Eventually, we even started taking nap breaks back at the hotel during mid-afternoon, when lines are longest. That helped, but the lines were still long.

Disney frequently surveys their guests, and for years the biggest complaint was about standing in line.

Finally, they did something about it.

Computer technology reached the point that FastPass could be developed. The FastPass term is trademarked, and Disney's implementation is patented, so you won't want to copy it, even if you run a theme park.

But the idea is simple. Find a way to help people utilize your products easier, faster, and in a way that's more fun.

The significance of an overflowing trash can

"Yuck," I thought. Then, because I'm me, I took a picture.

I was walking down the street in the Hollywood Pictures Backlot at Disney's California Adventure. A trash can standing beside a sidewalk cafe was overflowing trash, with trash spilling out onto the street.

I'd seen that before. In fact, it's a common sight at most fast food restaurants. You've seen it, too.

But in years of visiting, and looking at how things run, it's the first time I'd seen it in a Disney theme park. I've taken pictures of lots of trash cans at Disney parks. Not until this one day had I found one that was full, let alone overflowing.

It's notable by it's exception.

Before Disneyland, Walt Disney liked to spend a day on the weekend to take his daughters to amusement parks.

"When I started on Disneyland," Walt said, "my wife used to say, 'But why do you want to build an amusement park? They're so dirty.' I told her that was just the point – mine wouldn't be."

Walt vowed that Disneyland will be clean.

On opening day, Disneyland drew far more guests than expected. Trash piled up and it wasn't a pretty sight.

Disney took moves to clean the place up and to keep it clean. He made sure there were plenty of cleanup staff to clean up quickly. He ordered a trash can every 25 feet so guests could easily dispose of their trash. And he insisted that picking up trash was everyone's job. Even Walt would pick up trash.

"If you keep a place clean," Walt said, "people will respect it; if you let it get dirty, they'll make it worse."

This was more than the ranting of a creative genius. Walt wanted to create a storybook environment for his guests, and that didn't include trashy walkways or dirty corners.

So, today you'll still find trash cans about every 25 feet. And plenty of staff on hand to keep things clean. And everyone picks up trash.

And trash cans are emptied throughout the day.

Clean is a fundamental Disney value.

While the backstage areas, those places that guests never see, may not be decorated or themed like the onstage areas, they are clean.

Disney knew that it was important to create a clean environment so the cast would be happier and that, in turn, makes the guests happy.

I'm not telling you that you have to clean up your workplace, but you really might think about it. Employees see it. Your customers see it. It matters.

Prepare for 'situations'

"You have a lot of radios plugged into your ear for a pin trader," I told a Disney cast member in Tomorrowland.

While I was writing *Disney Magic,* I found her walking through Tomorrowland, talking with guests, answering questions, and giving directions.

I asked her, "What, exactly, is your job here?"

"I'm a pin trader," she answered.

I asked her about pin trading, and she explained how the pin trading program works.

Then I asked about the radios plugged in her ear. "Somehow it seems odd that a pin trader would need to stay in touch by radio," I said.

"Well," she answered, "if an attraction breaks down or some other situation develops, they contact me by radio so I can immediately go assist unloading guests from an attraction, making special arrangements, or whatever might be necessary."

That's when I discovered that a certain number of cast members are set up in noncritical jobs, like pin trading, so they can be onstage and ready to assist anywhere in the park when needed.

Disney is wise enough to know that problems will occur, and they want to be ready to respond when it happens.

The pin trader was ready to switch into rescue mode at a moments' notice. It meant that each attraction didn't have to retain enough staff to provide those services. It's a combination of preparedness and good economics.

It seems like a good idea. Be ready with staff who can switch to rescue mode at any time without negatively affecting the rest of the business.

Seeking a Fantasyland trash can pin

Pin trading is an activity that Disney discovered almost by accident.

They sold lapel pins at Disneyland from opening day, and a variety of pins has been produced for guests and cast members.

But around 1998 they saw active trading of Disney pins on the internet, and realized a new opportunity.

In 1999 they made pin trading an attraction at the theme parks and, for a time, at the Disney Store.

They started producing and selling far more pins.

They "seed" the operation with "free" pins, by organizing promotions through the Walt Disney Travel Company and AAA, giving each visitor to the resorts a special pin collector lanyard and a selection of pins. The pins are given in duplicate, so the guest can keep one and trade the other. That introduces thousands of people to the concept who wouldn't be aware of it otherwise.

Some pins are released in "limited editions." Though the limit is often in the thousands, sometimes they release only a few hundred, creating real scarcity.

They created a number of special pin series, at one point releasing five pins a week for a year. Customers lined up every Saturday morning in the malls to get into the Disney Store for a chance to buy those pins.

At the theme parks, pins used to be sold at a counter in the stores. Now they have added several kiosks in each park to sell pins, and pins are sold at other locations as well.

"Surprise" pins are released in the theme parks with no announcement, and you have to be lucky enough to be at the right location in the park when the pin is released, and savvy enough to make the buy. When it happens, the word spreads quickly among pin trading guests. (And other guests, not "in the know" about pin trading, don't even see it happening.)

Special pin trading areas are set up where guests can trade pins with other guests, and guests can trade with participating cast members, too. Those cast members wear special lanyards loaded with a variety of Disney pins.

Some of the cast members' pins are "exclusives," which means they were designed and manufactured for cast members only. Cast member pins are used in three ways:

1. Certain pins are provided to cast members who work "onstage" in the park as pin traders. These pins are traded with guests in exchange for other Disney pins. That means that if you want one of these exclusive pins, you must have (or buy) a Disney pin and then find a cast member who has the exclusive pin on their lanyard available to trade. Some of these are limited editions and may be available only for a few hours, or for one day.

2. Another series of pins is made available for various celebrations and cast member parties. For example, there may be a pin for the Disneyland anniversary that is given to each cast member. The Cast Member summer party is a big event, and special pins are often created and given out. Other parties get similar pins. Pins are made for cast members who work various holidays, like the Fourth of July or New Year's Eve. Still more pins are created for awarding to cast members providing special guest service or achieving other goals.

3. Cast member "exclusives" are also made and sold at the special backstage Disney stores where only cast members may shop. Each location has special pins; cast members at the Imagineering location in Glendale, California, will be able to buy different pins than the ones at Disneyland or Walt Disney World.

You'll find pins from the last two groups for sale on eBay, and traded by guests in the parks at pin trading locations. Cast members don't always keep the pins made especially for them.

Certainly it's hard to come up with an endless supply of designs for all these pins. Most are variations of Mickey, Minnie, or other Disney cartoon characters, in different situations. Some depict rides or buildings at the theme parks. There are pins commemorating pin trading.

They've even created pins depicting the trash cans around Disneyland. And they have made pins that commemorate the anniversaries of the Disneyland administration building, something you'll probably never see.

On a recent visit, they were running a Disney pin "scavenger hunt." Guests could get a master map-card when they came into the park. Then they trekked to each location on the map to pick up a special postcard and where they had the opportunity to buy a special pin. Finally, after collecting all the cards (and pins) they went to a final location where they were awarded a special pin. Each pin in the program was unique to the promotion that one day, available for only a very limited time.

So, what's the point?

First, they've capitalized on the collector market by creating lots of pins and by establishing places to trade pins. It all generates demand for more pins.

Second, they've created a new attraction for the parks, at very low cost. After all, if you pay fifty dollars to get in and spend eight hours at Disneyland, you're paying over six dollars an hour just to be there. If you spend an hour and a half trading pins, you're buying pins and you're reducing the demand on other, more expensive attractions. It's a brilliant marketing strategy.

What are you already doing in *your* business that can be expanded to be more fun and more profitable?

Remember your goal is to entertain your customer. Is there something you can expand to make the shopping experience more fun and build business at the same time?

When the Disney merchandisers came up with the pin trading program, they added exclusive pins for cast members to trade with guests.

Why not just sell them directly to the guests and be done with it?

Because this adds to the "attraction," and makes it more fun. You *have to* trade if you want all the pins. And you *have to explore the park* looking for surprise pins.

Somewhere, buried in *your* business, is a similar idea just waiting for your discovery. Watch your customers and see if they are already enjoying something in a way you didn't expect. Like Disney, you may find a new profit center and an opportunity to entertain your customers.

Cooking with Mickey

In 1987, Disney created a cookbook titled, *Cooking with Mickey.* It was billed as containing "the most popular recipes from Walt Disney World and Disneyland."

Bound with a big plastic comb binding, it was sold in stores in the theme parks and Disney hotels. The book was snatched up by people who enjoyed some of the special treats at the better Disney restaurants.

In 1994, the same book was reissued as *Mickey's Gourmet Cookbook,* and released to bookstores.

Earlier, the Mickey Mouse Cookbook had been published. About one-third the size of the later volumes, it had fewer recipes.

And for kids, they have *Cooking with Mickey and Friends,* featuring "more than 30 recipes for kids. Easy to make and even easier to eat!"

So what's the great idea here?

You can find additional products and services to sell right where you are. Disney had restaurants turning out meals. People even asked for recipes. They put together a cookbook and turned the request for a recipe into another profit center.

Some restaurants might be afraid they would lose customers if their special recipes were sold in the book. Not Disney! They recognized the bigger value in promotion. And they don't give away all the secrets, just a few.

It was more than a profit center. Every time someone uses a Mickey Mouse cookbook, they're reminded of Disneyland and Walt Disney World. Their friends see the cookbook and are reminded of the Disney theme parks, too.

Each recipe shows which restaurant and theme park featured the treat.

So, it's great public relations and great advertising, promoting the parks and the better restaurants. Cooks keep Mickey Mouse out on the kitchen counter! And they pay Disney to do it.

Should you put out a cookbook? Maybe. You don't have to run a restaurant to know about good recipes. You could grab your favorite recipes and put them together with an interesting story and create a recipe book with interesting stories *and* recipes.

What if a cookbook just doesn't make sense? Look closer. There are certainly a number of other powerful products that you can create out of your existing business, to create things to sell to your existing customers.

You can also license products or purchase them at wholesale to offer your customers.

For example, you could offer the *Disney Magic* book. If any of your customers run businesses or work in businesses (which, of course, is almost everybody), *Disney Magic* could be a real treat. It's short and easy to read, and full of useful ideas for use at work and at home. And it would give you an opportunity to *extend your business* and provide value to your customers beyond the level expected.

Unexpected value could be demonstrated by the very fact that offering a "business" book might seem out of character for your business type.

These same products might be used as a "prospecting" sale, something that is purchased and is then the basis for establishing a relationship with your new customer, leading to additional business.

Next time you visit Walt Disney World or Disneyland, look around. They make products out of everything!

And the beat goes on...

It's easy to think of Disney products as plush toys and sweatshirts. They certainly sell a lot of those.

Disney doesn't stop at cookbooks, either.

They sell Mickey Mouse waffle irons, sandwich makers, napkins, plates, and all kinds of kitchen accessories.

They have a store selling holiday decorations year round.

Another sells blown and cut or engraved glass.

They sell jewelry, watches, toys, pencils, erasers, books, and magic tricks.

In their clothing line you'll find far more than sweatshirts and t-shirts. They carry clothing for children and adults, even dress shirts with a small Mickey embroidered on the pocket. They carry golf clothes and nightshirts.

For girls they offer costumes so they can play dress up and be a princess.

Not everything on sale at a Disney Resort carries the Disney brand. They offer other quality products in addition to their own brand.

What about quality and value?

Just as Disney is known for quality in developing attractions, they insist on quality from the vendors that supply the products.

I compared their shirts to shirts on sale at a department store in the mall. Disney's price was lower. I checked a discount store. Disney's price was higher. My conclusion? They maintain a competitive mid-range price.

Disney maintains a high quality-value offering with products that are outside the mainstream definition of their business.

How does this apply to you?

Few businesses can survive on a single sale to a customer. It's the repeat and add-on sales that carry the profits for the enterprise.

Think about areas where you can add products to your offering.

It's best if you can maintain a "relationship" between the products and your main product or service. But it doesn't have to be a strong link. Only one that people can accept.

Most (not all) of the products found for sale at Disneyland and Walt Disney World carry a Disney character, logo, or imprint. That's important to Disney because they're marketing the Disney mystique.

Your situation is a little different.

A Mickey Mouse waffle iron is a neat idea. We've fixed Mickey Mouse waffles in our own kitchen.

But I wouldn't be so interested in an Acme Landscaping waffle. Well, a tree-shaped waffle might be interesting, but not the Acme logo.

So we're not suggesting you buy a bunch of advertising specialty products and stamp your name on them.

Instead, think of new product lines that you can introduce that will excite your customers. Ask *them* if they would be interested. If they are, make it part of your business.

Our fictional Acme Landscaping might be able to offer books on gardening and landscaping, and even a special cookbook featuring recipes that use vegetables you can grow in your home garden.

They could sell seeds, garden tools, and supplies. And they could deliver to the home while they're onsite mowing the lawn and trimming the trees.

They could even partner with a catering service to supply food catered for parties, using the Acme name.

Is that going to cut into their landscaping service business? Probably not; the people who will pay for that service, will still contract it. Some will buy both ways. The books, seeds, and supplies will all promote Acme and establish the company as dominant in their business.

You can apply these ideas to your business as well.

Outrageous hats and mouse ears

A trip to the Disney theme park reveals an interesting quirk of human behavior.

People who wouldn't be caught wearing a silly hat in public buy giant Mad Hatter hats, Mickey Mouse ears, fuzzy bug antennae, and other strange headwear and wear them throughout the park.

I often wonder what people do with this strange headwear when they go home. You certainly don't see them wearing it at the mall! (I keep my Indian Jones Adventure hat on the rear window shelf of one of my cars for the world to see... but not on my head except when I return to Disneyland.)

The answer is simple. They went to the Magic Kingdom for amusement, and while there, reality is suspended. Others are wearing silly hats and it seems like fun, so they buy a hat and they wear it for fun... while they're there.

What I hope you grasp is this:

I'm not suggesting you should sell silly hats at your place of business. It probably won't work. Remain reasonably practical.

At the same time, remember Walt Disney had the ability to be outrageous.

He could see what people would like and create an atmosphere where they could let loose of reality and participate in their own fantasy. It's part of what makes the park fun.

You, too, can be an outrageous thinker. Apply the mental energy to your business and think about what you can do to entertain your customer and be a little outrageous!

So many kiosks

"Just a minute, I want to get an apple," she said.

Sharon buys the healthy foods from the food carts. I buy the junk.

Throughout the Disney theme parks are kiosks, food carts, and refreshment stands, making it easy to buy something to eat or drink. They sell turkey legs, chimichangas, churros, popcorn, ice cream, french fries, soft drinks, and more.

Some carts even sell regular merchandise, including pins, personalized merchandise, and shirts.

In New Orleans Square, artists paint caricatures and cut silhouettes for guests.

It's more than convenience; it creates an impulse buy in a relaxed, open air atmosphere. You spend money without going into a store or restaurant.

It almost seems like the money, and the calories, don't count.

Churros

When is the last time you had a churro outside a Disney theme park?

Chances are, unless you got it from Disney, you haven't eaten a churro.

And just in case you don't remember churros, they're those long sticks of deep fried dough, rolled in cinnamon sugar, sold at churro carts all around the Magic Kingdom.

Churros are sold in Spain from churrería stands, usually without the cinnamon and with a chocolate dip instead. But that would be too messy for Disneyland.

A major Hispanic dessert pastry, churros are often found in Mexico, at fairs where people may stand in line for hours waiting to buy a churro.

Churros began their road to "American" recognition in amusement parks, circuses, country fairs, and swap meets.

At Disneyland they serve them hot and fresh, rolled in sugar as you watch, and they're a tasty treat.

The American Heritage Dictionary describes a churro as "a thick coiled fritter of fried dough." To me it's just a long donut, sold for about three dollars.

They *are* tasty, though, and fun to eat. Not really unique to Disney, they help establish the unique, festive atmosphere that Disney wants you to experience.

This is another example of a surprise you get at the Disney theme parks. You didn't really go there to buy a churro. But you wouldn't want to leave without getting at least one.

Isn't there something unique you can add to *your* business that would be a warm pleasant surprise?

Remember, the idea is to give your customer another chance to smile. How about a unique treat, unexpected at your kind of business?

California Churros

When I went over to Disney's California Adventure park, I saw they had churro stands there, too. Just like at Disneyland.

But wait, the sign is different.

It reads, "California Churros."

At Disneyland the signs read, simply, "Churros."

So what's the difference between a California Churro at Disney's California Adventure and a Churro at Disneyland?

The sign. One is at Disney's California Adventure and the other is at Disneyland.

Is this really an opportunity to market the "California" emphasis at DCA, or is it just a touch of a sense of humor?

Probably both.

And can't you do the same thing?

Doesn't it make sense to have multiple versions of certain products and to label them appropriately so they're better identified with the various target audiences you want to reach?

A special treat from guest relations

"I'm sorry, there's been a breakdown on Indiana Jones. It probably won't be open the rest of the day," the smiling guest relations cast member said. "Your FastPass ticket won't do any good unless they open the ride. Will you be coming back tomorrow?"

It was after sundown at Disneyland, and we were leaving the next morning. We were disappointed that we wouldn't be able to ride Indy, and we probably looked pretty glum.

Cast members are trained to turn glum moments into magic moments, and this specialist picked it right up.

"Let me give you readmission passes," she said. "I can't make Indian Jones run for you, since it's broken down, but you can use these at any other attraction in the park, and you won't have to wait in line."

I call them line-cut passes.

They create an immediate morale boost.

With these cards we can go ride Splash Mountain, or Space Mountain, or anything else, and not have to wait in line.

For Disney, there's practically no cost, beyond printing the coupons.

And the guest gets special attention with a high perceived value. (I wish I had a whole *box* of those coupons!)

How about your business?

What is there in your business that you can do to give a customer special attention that costs next to nothing? A certificate for free rush service on their next order? A coupon for 10% free on their next job? A special phone number that rings to someone who can solve their problems faster?

It's a party in Town Square!

The Mad Hatter was recruiting guests in Town Square to join the "Disneyland Chorus" and sing with the Disneyland Band.

He made a big production of it. I don't remember that there was much singing, but I watched little girls (and their mothers) dance with the Mad Hatter and everyone had a good time.

The characters are often hamming it up, but there's more fun at every turn.

California churros, funny hats, and hidden Mickeys. All are examples of the Disney Imagineers and merchandisers making a clever joke about their work, a hidden message for you to catch and notice.

Remember, Walt Disney wanted people to leave with a smile on their face.

A good, positive sense of humor makes that possible.

And it carries throughout the property.

Unexpected magic

One of the slickest ways to create a magic moment is to give your customer or prospective customer a surprise.

You probably go to Disneyland to ride the rides.

And the first surprise you get is the beautiful landscaping. Just inside the entrance on a hillside is a giant image of Mickey Mouse, planted in beautiful, colorful flowers. At every turn you discover lush green trees and flower beds brimming with color.

Throughout Disneyland you hear beautiful music, piped in through a high quality stereo sound system. The music is selected to match the locale and the time of day.

Walking down Main Street you may encounter a barbershop quartet, performing 1900-era songs.

In the "hub" you may find the Disneyland Band.

And in New Orleans Square, look for a jazz combo.

These all delight the guests at Disneyland. Yet few, if any, went there for landscaping or musical treats.

What can you give *your guests* that will surprise them, treating them with *something unexpected?*

Susan is a friend of mine who sells real estate. Over the years, she has tried all the conventional "gifts" for her clients, including pens, magnets, and real estate shopping planners.

When she saw my *Disney Magic* book, she told me that she had considered a number of different books about real estate for her clients, but most of them seemed too dry and didn't really convey the image she wanted to project.

But *Disney Magic* gave her an idea. Because it's a book that is written with success concepts for business managers, employees, and for people at home, she saw it as a gift that would be a complete surprise. When I told her she could buy them wholesale in case lots, she actually got excited.

The show after the show

The Star Tours exit lets out into the Star Traders store.

It's a Small World exits into a small toy store.

Jungle Cruise exits next to a jungle trader store, complete with very realistic rubber snakes. And across from the exit is another animal-themed store.

Splash Mountain exits to a gallery of photographs taken of you while on the ride.

At Disney theme parks, they never miss the opportunity to let you buy something. And part of that strategy is creating pathways that lead you right to the shopping area.

Even the Disneyland exit is through Main Street USA; the stores are open late and are very busy late in the day as people leave.

This can be a challenge in some situations.

Still, it pays to give people plenty of opportunity to discover things they might want, without creating a confusing maze that makes it hard for them to get where they need to go.

At the grocery store or the discount store, while you wait to check out, there's a four or five-foot rack of merchandise tempting you for an impulse sale. Clever? Yes, and profitable.

A large electronics store near my home goes one better. They have over 30 registers, with one long checkout line that feeds all the registers. That checkout line, probably 150 feet long, is bordered with merchandise displays. While the line seems long, it moves pretty fast because there are lots of registers. And every customer is exposed to a variety of impulse offerings, from candy bars and snacks to batteries and music CDs.

An afterthought that made it all work

Disneyland and the Disneyland Hotel have been linked in the mind of the public since Disneyland's first year.

But it wasn't always part of the plan.

In fact, Disneyland construction was well underway when Walt Disney realized that if he was going to make Disneyland a *destination* with visitors from all over the country, he needed a hotel facility so people would have a place to stay.

When Walt realized that, he had already spent all of the Disneyland construction money; there was no money for a hotel.

So he turned to his friend, Jack Wrather, producer of Lassie and Rin Tin Tin. Walt pitched Wrather on the idea of building a hotel next to Disneyland. It was a tough sell, because Wrather thought building a hotel out in the middle of nowhere was a crazy idea.

Finally, he agreed, building a small motel, expanding it, and discovering rather quickly that Disneyland really would support a full hotel.

Walt was grateful, and thought this was a significant reason for Disneyland's success.

A few years later, when he expanded the Monorail line outside the park, he made the outside station at the front of the Disneyland Hotel, strengthening the hotel's marketing position, as a thank you to Wrather.

Wrather Corporation continued to run the Disneyland Hotel until the 80's when Disney purchased the operation.

The hotel made Disneyland a destination, viable for a nationwide, even worldwide, market. It's a prime example of partnering; Walt was convinced that without the hotel, Disneyland would not become a world-class attraction. And the hotel was just another hotel without Disney.

Who are Disney's best customers?

"Disney employees are Disney's best customers." I first heard that from a Disney Store employee, and since then I've witnessed intense interest in Disney products by theme park employees.

Disney encourages it, giving discounts of up to 30% on Disney merchandise to cast members.

And they built special stores for the cast, often called "Company D" stores.

They also create special merchandise for sale to cast members only. This includes everything from stadium cushions to sweatshirts, jackets, and lanyards to display employee id cards.

Sometimes this special merchandise shows up on eBay, often selling above list price because of its special limited cast issue. I've heard cast members say that reselling cast merchandise would be wrong, but in the end it's just another sales channel.

After your theme park adventure, shop and have dinner

Originally, Disneyland had contract restaurants like Don Defore's Frontierland eatery.

Over time, Disney took over all food services, because Walt wanted control to maintain high quality and reasonable prices.

With the expansion at the Disneyland Resort, Disney took an approach already in use at Walt Disney World. While Disney controlled much of the in-park eateries, many of the on-property but out of park locations were leased to other companies.

Now at the Disneyland Resort's "Downtown Disney," you'll find a number of independent restaurants. Disney gets a cut, and people stay on the Disney property longer.

How Disneyland makes money before they open

When Disneyland opens at 9am, they usually open the gates 45 minutes to an hour earlier, at 8:00 or 8:15.

Guests are admitted to the Main Street USA area, and the far end of Main Street is blocked until actual opening.

This gives the guests someplace nice to wait, better than the parking lot or ticketing area. It functions much like the pre-show area of an attraction.

And while they're there, guests can have breakfast and shop in the Main Street stores.

Promotion, free advertising, and paid advertising

This one I didn't see at Disneyland or Walt Disney World; I saw it before I left home: Television ads that made me want to plan my trip to the Disney theme parks.

It seemed like a contrast to Walt Disney's main concept to promote the park, the use of cross promotion and free advertising.

Cross promotion

One of the most powerful things Disney did at Disneyland was create attractions based on his movies, television programs, and cartoons.

Attractions like Snow White's Scary Adventure, Mr. Toad's Wild Ride, and the Davy Crockett Explorer Canoes all tied to a theatrical production. In fact, nearly every attraction did.

Exceptions, like Pirates of the Caribbean and the Haunted Mansion were turned into movies later by the Disney Studios. The Pirates movie was a big hit, and the theme park attraction was a real asset in creating public opinion.

Roy Disney, Walt's brother and business partner, said, "We don't do anything in one line without giving a thought to its likely profitability in other lines."

It's good advice for any business.

Make one purchase lead to another related product.

Free advertising

Nearly a year before Disneyland opened, the weekly *Disneyland* television program, hosted by Walt Disney himself, started presenting a variety of features. Four hour-long programs the first year were about the construction and development at Disneyland. Many of the other programs, however interesting, were blatant promotional vehicles.

The public ate it up; they wanted to know more!

The lesson here is that it pays to use free advertising.

In Walt's case, the company was paid to produce the program. That won't happen for most people, but well thought out publicity efforts can result in news features and radio or television programs or interviews that can have a greater impact than any paid advertising.

Of course, it's harder, if not impossible, to control publicity. And that brings us to the third area, paid advertising.

Paid advertising

Walt avoided buying paid advertising as much as possible, and the company was able to start and operate Disneyland without any significant advertising budget.

Eventually, the media market changed, with hundreds of cable tv channels, more radio stations, and more complex listenership and viewership patterns.

While it was foolish to buy advertising during the first three decades of the Disney theme park operations, that changed.

In 1984, a test campaign was run on local television channels in Chicago and Houston. The results indicated that for every million dollars spent on television advertising, an additional 154,000 guests would visit the park. They figured that a ten million dollar campaign would result in over 55 million in revenues.

Following the successful test, an ad campaign was put together for both Disneyland and Walt Disney World. And advertising has continued since.

The lesson is clear; paid advertising can be very effective if it's targeted in the right media, and if proper testing is done to determine effectiveness before major expenditures are made.

An online money-making machine

Walt Disney would have embraced the internet.

Yes, Walt died in 1966. So how do I know Walt would embrace the internet?

Because Walt was an innovator. He was the first to add sound to animated cartoons, the first to create a color cartoon, and the first to create a feature length animated movie. Disneyland was another innovation, as were his ideas for EPCOT in Florida.

And today, the Disney company actively utilizes the internet in many ways.

You can buy theme park tickets online. Make a reservation at a Disney hotel. Buy Disney merchandise. Buy movies. Play online computer games.

Disney has expanded it's online presence in amazing ways. Check it out at www.Disney.com.

And that's just the beginning. They use special websites for special programs and activities, for news media relations, and for cast member support.

What is the Internet?

First, let's deal with what the internet is *not*. The internet is not a magic replacement for good business sense.

The dot-com crash of 2000-2002 proved that. In the five years leading up to that crash, the internet grew rapidly, but business speculators invested lavishly and unwisely in business models that suggested the internet would take over commerce.

While dot-com companies were going broke, and stocks were diving, some companies succeeded. A very few created a unique internet business that survived and thrived. Most of the successes came from companies who used the internet as an additional channel or tool to parallel or support their existing successful business.

Even Disney unwisely jumped in and acquired go.com, with unrealistic expectations. Ultimately, they shut down most of the go.com operation, and turned it into a central Disney *service and support site*. As I write this, at go.com you'll see information and links to the various Disney divisions and activities. It's evolved into a remarkable resource.

So what is the internet? It's another channel for doing business. It's a tool to enhance your business.

It's...

A computer network. You use computers to automate your business so certain things are done quickly, accurately, and cheaply. By linking your computers with many others, you save money and improve customer service.

A communications network. Email is the front line in using the internet as a communications tool. Other reporting systems and interactivity tools expand communications between employees and with customers. Online training and customer surveys automate certain aspects of the communications process. Some companies are even switching telephone service to the internet.

An information network. Your website can contain information useful to customers, prospective customers, and employees. Search engines make it possible to locate information you would not find otherwise. Links between sites lead you to even more information.

A transaction network. The network is capable of handling financial transactions with reasonable security and even delivering some products and services (information products, airline tickets, movie tickets, etc.)

Further information

In my book, *Internet Business Magic,* I go into detail about some of the internet strategies you can use to create a powerful internet business based on the principles we've learned from Walt Disney.

For a second chance, eBay

Is there something you didn't buy last time you visited Disneyland? Or, was there something you thought about buying, but they didn't have it when you went back?

Lots of discontinued Disney merchandise is sold by Disney on eBay, often at about half price.

I bought a warm lined Disneyland jacket during one visit, when the weather was colder than I'd expected. The jacket was $75, a reasonable price for a good quality jacket.

The following winter, the same jacket was on sale on eBay for half the price. It was brand new, being sold by Disney.

By that time at Disneyland they had a similar jacket, but with slightly different decoration. So the old jacket was discontinued merchandise.

Disney also sells art on eBay. You'll find discontinued prints, artwork removed from the Disney hotels, and promotional art originally developed for the theme parks.

They even sell their junk on eBay, figuring someone will see the old trade show booth as a valuable Disney artifact.

You could do that, too, at very low cost. Set up an auction program on eBay to sell your discontinued and returned merchandise. There's an international market out there on the internet, and for the most part, it won't affect your regular sales.

Partners make a bigger enterprise

It was a puzzle in 1953. Walt Disney was trying to figure out how to pay for his dream project, Disneyland.

Suddenly he put the project together with another opportunity.

For some years, the television networks had been trying to lure Disney (and other movie producers) into creating product for television. Most had refused, but Walt had experimented with a couple of television specials.

Struggling to find the money to develop Disneyland, Walt reasoned television was the answer. In return for an investment in Disneyland, Walt would agree to create regular Disney programming for the participating television network.

CBS and NBC declined, but the new ABC network jumped at the chance. In a short time ABC had the programming they wanted: a weekly Disney feature program *(Disneyland)*, a new series *(Zorro)*, and a daily children's program *(The Mickey Mouse Club)*. All three were hits.

ABC also held a large ownership interest in the new Disneyland park. They sold it back to Disney a few years later at a handsome profit, at a time when Disney had more cash due in great part to Disneyland.

I think it ironic that 40 years later Disney bought ABC.

This major partnering effort between ABC and Disney made Disneyland possible.

Since that time Disney has enhanced the park, reduced the risk, or increased the revenue through many partnering and sponsorship arrangements.

For the 1964 World's Fair in New York, Disney created four major attractions for four key partners: General Electric, Ford, Pepsi-Cola, and the State of Illinois. After the fair, all or part of those attractions were relocated to Disneyland, giving the park It's a Small World, Circle of Progress, Great Moments with Mr. Lincoln, and the Grand

Canyon and Primeval World features on the Disneyland Railroad. Leftover prehistoric creatures from the Ford exhibit showed up years later in the energy exhibit at Epcot.

Walt had figured out how to get corporate America to pay for the development of major attractions in the park, including the development of technology he needed for future attractions like Enchanted Tiki Room, Pirates of the Caribbean and Haunted Mansion. Audio animatronics, the PeopleMover system, and the technology that made Carousel of Progress possible all came out of this venture.

Disney even discovered special talent. General Joe Potter worked with the Army Corps of Engineers for many years and was one of the key people on the Fair's staff. Disney hired Potter away from the Fair as it was winding down, and ultimately put him in charge of construction at the Florida project, the future Walt Disney World.

Other examples of partnering include development of the Disneyland Hotel by the Wrather Corporation and leasing certain restaurants and retail outlets on the park property.

Does this apply to other businesses and organizations that don't have Disney's huge crowds?

I remember when I was young going to Leonida's Restaurant for dinner. Leonida's was a small, family restaurant in a downtown location next to a movie theatre. They were busy at lunch but the dinner traffic was light.

So Leonida's partnered with the movie theatre, and offered a movie ticket with each dinner on certain nights. They advertised "dinner and a movie" at a low combination price. Their ads promoted the current movie features, and the theatre provided tickets at a low price in return for the advertising. Both companies came out winners.

Sponsorship allows other firms to participate in your business

Beyond partnering, Disney has used extensive sponsoring to boost revenues and give other firms exposure to Disney's guests.

And you thought "sponsoring" meant buying advertising on radio or television programs. It's much more than that!

The bank that financed many of Disney's movies and other projects, Bank of America, had either a branch office or ATM facilities inside Disneyland for nearly 45 years.

The Santa Fe & Disneyland Railroad circled the new Disneyland in 1955. It was renamed Disneyland Railroad when the Santa Fe sponsorship ended in 1972.

Other early sponsorships included the Dutch Boy Paint Color Gallery, Carnation Ice Cream Parlor, Hills Bros. Coffee House and Gardens, Kaiser's Hall of Aluminum Fame, Monsanto Hall of Chemistry, Upjohn Pharmacy, Sunkist Citrus House, Sunkist I Presume, Global Van Lines Locker Service, Hallmark Communications Center, INA Carefree Corner, Swift's Red Wagon Inn, Wurlitzer Music Hall, and Yale & Towne Lock Shop.

Rocket to the Moon was presented by TWA, and later by Douglas Aircraft Co. Goodyear sponsored PeopleMover. Richfield sponsored Autopia.

Different pet food brands have sponsored Disneyland's pet boarding facility. The original sponsor was Ken-L Ration. Later sponsors were Kal Kan, Gaines, Friskies, and Purina.

Eastman Kodak has long been a sponsor at Disneyland, but that was interrupted in the 1970s when GAF was the official film of Disneyland. If it's true that four percent of the pictures taken in the USA are taken in a Disney theme park, this is probably a powerful sponsorship investment.

Pepsi-Cola sponsored Disneyland's Golden Horseshoe Saloon until 1982, resulting in lots of Pepsi-Cola being sold at Disneyland.

In Disneyland's souvenir schedule from the 1960's, the listing for the Golden Horseshoe Saloon read, "No alcohol is served in this saloon, which is underwritten by Pepsi-Cola... Pepsi-Cola is the most powerful beverage allowed at Disneyland."

Today, you'll find Coca-Cola signs (and Coca-Cola for sale) all over the park, and you'll find Refreshment Corner, "hosted by Coca-Cola."

This is only a small part of the sponsorship story. The point is that many, if not most, of Disney's attractions, stores, and activities are sponsored by someone looking to reach all those guests.

It makes sense that sponsors would want to promote to Disney's huge crowds, but would a sponsor be interested in a smaller business, or a large business that doesn't generate heavy traffic?

When the business deal is right, it will work.

Carole Copeland Thomas runs "empowerment breakfasts" where she acts as host and a guest speaker presents the featured program. She sells sponsorships to the hotel where the event is held, to banks, to restaurants, and to real estate companies.

I know a professional photographer who presents training programs for other pros across the country every year. The program is priced moderately, and it's well advertised so there's always a big turnout. He sells sponsorships to various industry suppliers, who provide the equipment he uses in his training. The sponsorship fees pay for the advertising, travel, and meeting rooms, and the sponsors also provide their mailing lists for promotion. He pockets the admission fees and sells additional training materials to attendees.

Kodak often has special programs for portrait studios and camera dealers that display the Kodak logo and use Kodak products. It usually involves supplying high quality promotional materials at a low cost.

The Kodak programs are "standard" sponsorship programs, but unique sponsorships may be created if the idea and implementation is right. (Disney is ample proof of that.)

There's a reason that you see the Coca-Cola logo printed on the paper cups and most of the signs at McDonald's and Burger King. It's because Coca-Cola is more than a supplier; they "participate" in the promotions and advertising because it helps sell more of their product.

Sometimes sponsorship will be a cash investment in return for exposure or inclusion in a product or service, and sometimes it's another kind of business involvement, leaning more towards a partnership of sorts, sometimes called a "joint venture."

Here's the challenge. How can you start to compartmentalize your business in ways that would lend themselves to sponsorship or participation by a supplier or a complementary firm?

Maybe there's a way to promote someone else's business to your customers while they promote your business to their customers. That might provide you both with the opportunity for profit without a major cash outlay.

Consider sponsorship opportunities.

Disneyland's secret club

I was answering most of the trivia questions correctly. The internet quiz asked questions about Disneyland and Walt Disney World.

The question that caught me was this: "Is there is a secret club serving hard liquor in New Orleans Square, Disneyland?"

I knew the answer, of course. There is no such thing.

But I was wrong!

Tucked away in New Orleans Square is a very private, very exclusive club. It's called "Club 33," and its unmarked entrance is next door to the Blue Bayou Restaurant. It's said that opening the door requires a special electronic card.

An antique French lift transports guests to the dining area of Club 33, on the top floor above the Blue Bayou and Cafe Orleans restaurants.

I asked a cast member at the Disney Gallery about Club 33. She told me that it's real, a 5-star quality dining experience, and that Disney intends for it to be the finest dining experience in California.

As I was finishing this book, I visited with a former Disney Imagineer. He told me a coworker was fascinated with Club 33, but never found a member who could arrange a reservation. Finally he went to Marty Sklar, the head of Walt Disney Imagineering to see if Marty could arrange a reservation.

Marty did just that, and the coworker enjoyed a fabulous meal at Club 33.

"It sounded so wonderful," the Imagineer told me. "I figured that I'd never get to enjoy Club 33 myself." Then one day, after he left Disney, his wife received a call from a business acquaintance inviting them to join him at Club 33 the next day.

Club 33 retains exclusivity with a five-figure initiation fee, annual dues running into four-figures, and a long waiting list for membership. The posh private club serves gourmet food and fine wines and is the only place inside Disneyland where alcohol is served.

Standing across from the Blue Bayou entrance, you can watch arriving and departing guests, and get a glimpse inside the Victorian style entry. Watching can get pretty boring, but if you have the patience and watch for days you *might* see some celebrities. Club 33 is very secretive about their members and guests, but internet reports suggest Robert Wagner, Michael Jackson, Jack Nicholson, Kevin Costner, Tom Hanks, Geena Davis, and many others have been spotted there.

Club membership is limited to about 400. Most members are not celebrities, but are influential members of the business community.

When I took the Walk with Walt Tour, I asked the cast member guide, "Where is the best place to eat in Disneyland?"

He told me, "It's the Blue Bayou Restaurant."

"What about Club 33?" I asked.

"Well, yes, Club 33 would be *the* best place to eat in Disneyland, but we don't tell you about it because it's a private club, you can't go, and it's kind of a secret."

Since that time, they added a visit to Club 33 to the Walk with Walt Tour, but that "visit" is simply a peek into the entrance area.

There is no similar club at the Walt Disney World Resort or Disneyland Paris, but there is a Club 33 at Tokyo Disneyland.

How might this apply to your business?

I know a consultant who has a "Platinum Club," limited to 15 clients. They get very special treatment, recognition, and quarterly meetings with the consultant and other Platinum Club members who become a sort of "mind trust."

Years ago American Express established the Gold Card memberships for special, exclusive clients. When Gold Cards became common, they created the Platinum Card, with even higher requirements (and fees). Eventually, even that wasn't enough, and they added the Titanium Card as their top offering.

Consider a special club for special customers, providing very special privileges at a high cost. Keep it a secret, offering it only to your top customers, and "leaking" the secret to those who might be eligible in the future.

Fill your business with people who 'get it'

As I visit Disneyland and Walt Disney World, I am constantly amazed at the friendliness and helpfulness of the Disney cast members.

They're efficient, with thousands visiting the attractions daily. They're clean-cut, well-groomed, enthusiastic, and, coming from a diverse range of ethnic backgrounds, and each seems to project a positive "Disney look."

Much of this comes about because the Disney recruiting program is designed to hire people who already understand what Disney is about, at least to some degree.

Disney has one advantage that you probably can't enjoy in your business. The Disney theme parks are so big and well known that most applicants have visited as guests and have some idea of what to expect before they apply. It makes sense that most applicants would look around and think, "I can fit in here," before they apply.

In your firm, you'll probably need to spend some time with applicants describing the atmosphere, the culture, and what is expected.

The company encourages existing employees to refer friends and acquaintances by becoming "Casting Scouts." Certainly anyone recruited in this manner would already have a good idea of what the company expects, and they must think they would fit in or they wouldn't apply.

During the application process, applicants are told about the company rules and expectations. Disney makes it easy for applicants to drop out of the process right then.

The "Disney look" is no accident. Disney has a booklet titled *The Disney Look* that is provided to each cast member, describing what is expected and acceptable in terms of dress, hygiene, hairstyles, and personal grooming.

The idea is to hire people who "get it." The Disneyland Recruiting department attempts to find people who already understand what the company expects and who think they fit the expectation. Cast members are encouraged to become "recruiting scouts" and refer their friends as potential employees.

Then training is provided to reinforce and expand on that knowledge so cast members understand what is expected and what the company is trying to achieve.

You've heard the saying, "Misery loves company." When people stand around and gripe on the job it's a negative attitude that can spread very quickly.

At Disney, they look for positive enthusiasm. And they expect those chosen to spread a positive feeling throughout the enterprise.

It's a worthy idea for any company, including yours. Define what you're looking for, explain that to prospective employees, then hire people who already "get it."

Manage by example

Every Disney theme park employee learns this on the first day: "The park must be clean, and everyone picks up trash. The managers, even the presidents of Disneyland and Walt Disney World, will stop and pick up trash if they see it."

It sets the proper example for all cast members. Everyone picks up trash, and the parks, even backstage, stay clean.

As new cast members hear that story on the first day, they learn part of what is expected of them. When they go into the park and they see their manager pick up trash, it confirms what they've been told is true. And because others do it, even managers, they don't have any reluctance to do it themselves.

Most managers are not trained for all the jobs in the park. So it would be difficult to "set the example" across the board. For example, the Disneyland president probably does not know how to load riders on the Matterhorn. But she can set the example for the "common" tasks, maintaining a pleasant interaction with a guest, smiling and presenting a happy demeanor, and picking up trash.

It's an example of Disney's "manage by example" philosophy. It's better than managing by objectives or results, and worlds ahead of "managing by walking around." Further, Disney proves that it works.

I don't want to suggest that Disney doesn't set goals or objectives or that Disney managers don't walk around; that's simply not true.

They set standards for guest satisfaction and attraction capacity. In fact, they have procedures, standards, and objectives for every aspect of the operation. And they get out in the park to identify guest needs and to provide on-the-spot training for cast members.

They also encourage their managers and leads to spend time in the park as a guest, bringing their families and buying meals and merchandise like other guests, so they get a firsthand experience of what it's like to be a guest.

But the key to their success is that the managers set a good example. In the early years at Disneyland, the only surprise in seeing Walt Disney himself picking up trash would be that some other cast member hadn't picked it up first.

Cross-Shoe Training

"He means 'cross-training,'" I thought.

When I first heard a Disney executive talk about "cross-shoe training," I was sure I had heard him wrong.

At Disneyland and Walt Disney World, they do a lot of cross-training. After a cast member is experienced at one attraction, they will train him on another. This provides variety in his work and gives the company the advantage of an employee that may be utilized on more than one attraction. It's useful, and lots of companies do it.

Quickly I realized that I heard the term right after all. *Cross-shoe* training or cross-shoe time is time that salaried cast members get to learn a job different than their own. I remembered seeing a man cooking pancakes in the River Belle Restaurant. Nearly every pancake he cooked was thrown away by the staff. I asked the clerk if he was a Disney exec, getting his "day in the park," and she said yes.

Walt Disney didn't want an administration building at Disneyland, because he wanted his managers out in the park, working with attractions and talking to guests. Over time, this became the command: "Take a day or two in the park, a couple of times a year, to learn a new job. You'll gain insight into what cast members do and what guests are expecting."

Now they call that "cross-shoe." It's like cross training, but the purpose is to spend some time in the other person's shoes so you learn what she faces and what the guests she encounters are expecting.

Special assignment

At Disney's California Adventure I met a cast member working a theatre gate during a special Soap Opera event. I learned that he normally worked the Jungle Cruise in Disneyland.

As we talked, I told him that the night before I'd been on the Jungle Cruise and had the best ride ever. Talking a little longer, we realized that he was the energetic skipper of the boat I was on the night before. He was responsible for my special ride that night.

He was working the Soap Opera special event as "TDA," Temporary Duty Assignment. He was taking a day off his regular jungle duty to help the event and gain a day of non-routine work.

Like cross-training and cross-shoe, this broadens the abilities and understanding of the cast.

Now, go to Disneyland or Walt Disney World

One of the most interesting discoveries I've made is that most of the great things Disney does are common, everyday ideas. Except for Pin Trading, most every concept I've documented here is in use in other businesses.

The key difference is this: At Disney, they do all this very well, and *they do it all*. On one hand, everything is so simple. On the other hand, there's so much of it. How can you manage to get it all working for you?

Occasionally, I'm criticized for sugarcoating what I've found at the Disney theme parks. "It sounds so perfect," one man told me, "but I know there have been problems." That's true.

I'd like to suggest that my purpose here was to help you with powerful, successful ideas that you can use in your organization. I think I've done that. My purpose was to show you what to do, not what *not* to do.

It's also important to recognize that Disney doesn't always get it right the first time. Walt made many mistakes, but one of his keys to success was to evaluate and adapt, and to move on with his projects. It's a good lesson.

Your next move depends on your decision to commit. Make a list of all the ideas in this book that you can implement in some way. Then visit Disneyland or Walt Disney World and examine how these ideas are implemented. Ask cast members about them. Try them out.

Then return home and systematically apply them in your own business.

Help along the way

Since this book is intentionally thin, so that it's quick to read and easy to carry with you, it's necessary to provide you with additional resources to assist in your endeavors. I'm excited to be able to do that in a dynamic and adaptive way.

I want to stay in touch with you and help you achieve all your dreams, your goals, your desires. I also want you to share with me your success stories and let you read the stories of others. For this purpose we have created a special internet website:

www.MagicStrategy.com

To access the special section for readers who have finished the book click on the "Members" button. Your special access code is 1955. If you've paid attention, you'll remember the significance of that number, and that's why we used it as an access code.

This book is short; at the website you'll find additional information about using these methods.

This information will help you in countless ways, so keep your copy of this book close and refer to it often.

Share this information with others in your family, your company, your school, or your organization. As more people adopt these methods, the resulting synergy will create remarkable results.

Suggested Reading

Books and Audio

Adventures in Creative Thinking, audio by Mike Vance
Be Our Guest, book by the Disney Institute
Disney Magic: Business Strategy You Can Use at Work and at Home, book by Rich Hamilton
The Disney Version, book by Richard Schickel
The Disney Way, book by Bill Capodagli and Lynn Jackson
Inside the Dream: The Personal Story of Walt Disney, book by Katherine Barrett, Richard Greene, and Katherine Greene
Inside the Magic Kingdom: Seven Keys to Disney's Success, book by Tom Connellan
Internet Business Magic: Using Disney's Magic Strategy in Your Own Online Business, book by Rich Hamilton
The Magic Kingdom: Walt Disney and the American Way of Life, book by Steven Watts
The Man Behind the Magic: The Story of Walt Disney, book by Katherine Greene and Richard Greene
Mouse Tales: A Behind the Ears Look at Disneyland, book by David Koenig
Prince Of The Magic Kingdom: Michael Eisner And The Re-Making Of Disney, book by Joe Flower
Remembering Walt: Favorite Memories of Walt Disney, book by Amy Boothe Green and Howard E. Green
Walt Disney, book by Diane Disney Miller as told to Pete Martin
Walt Disney: An American Original, book by Bob Thomas
Walt Disney: Famous Quotes
Walt Disney Imagineering: A Behind the Dreams Look at Making the Magic Real, book by The Imagineers and C. E. Jones

Internet Resources

Disney Online: http://www.disney.com
Disneyland Inside & Out: http://www.intercotwest.com
Laughing Place: http://laughingplace.com
MiceAge: http://www.miceage.com
Mouse Planet: http://www.mouseplanet.com
Mike Vance: http://www.creativethinkingassoc.com
Special websites for readers of this book:
  http://www.MagicStrategy.com

Index

A

AAA 50
ABC 73–74
American Express 25, 80
annual passport 28–29
autograph books 30
Autopia 75

B

backpacks 30
Bank of America 75
barbershop quartet 63
Big Thunder Mountain
 Railroad 43
Blue Bayou 78, 79
books 31, 55
bottled water 31
breakfast 31
Broadway-style production 33
Burger King 77

C

Cafe Orleans 78
California churros 61
cameras 31
caricatures 59
Carnation Ice Cream
 Parlor 75
Carousel of Progress 74
carpet cleaning 37
cast members 14, 17
CBS 73
cell phone holsters 30
characters 30
chimichangas 59
churros 59, 60
Circle of Progress 74
classes 39
clean 15, 47–48
clothing 55
Club 33 77–78, 78
Coca-Cola 11, 76, 77
Cockerell, Lee 20
collector market 52
conversation 14
cookbook 53–54
Cooking with Mickey 53
Cooking with Mickey and
 Friends 53
core purpose 20–21
costumes 30, 55
credit cards 25, 35
cross-shoe training 83

D

Davy Crockett Explorer
 Canoes 68
Defore, Don 67
dinner 31
Disney Dollars 35–36
Disney Gallery 78
Disney image 11
Disney look 80
Disney University 17–19
Disneyland Band 62, 63
Disneyland Chorus 62
Disneyland Hotel 65, 74
Disneyland Look 17
Disneyland Railroad
 74, 75
Disneyland television
 program 69
Disney's Aladdin 33
dot-com crash 71
Douglas Aircraft Co. 75
Dutch Boy Paint Color
 Gallery 75

E

Eastman Kodak 75
eBay 72–73
empowerment breakfasts
 77
Enchanted Tiki Room 74
entertainers 14
entertainment business
 14–15
erasers 30, 55

F

FastPass 45, 62
Fill Your Jets 11
film 31
first name policy 17
flowers 63
Ford 74
french fries 59
friendly 15
Friskies 75

G

GAF 75
Gaines 75
General Electric 74
gift certificates 35
gifts 64
glass, cut and blown 55
Global Van Lines Locker
 Service 75
Gold Card 80
Golden Horseshoe Saloon
 75
Goodyear 75
Grand Canyon 74
Great Moments with Mr.
 Lincoln 41, 74
Grizzly River Run 42

H

Hallmark Communications Center 75
hats 58
Haunted Mansion 68, 74
headwear 58
hidden Mickey 38, 63
Hills Bros. Coffee House
 75
holiday decorations 55
Home Improvement 30

I

ice cream 59
Illinois, State of 74
INA Carefree Corner 75
Indiana Jones and the
 Temple of Doom 62
Indiana Jones and the
 Temple of the
 Forbidden Eye
 42, 43, 60
internet 69–71, 84
Internet Business Magic
 72
It's a Small World 64, 74

J

jazz combo 63
jewelry 55
Jim Henson 43
Jungle Cruise 64, 84

K

Kaiser's Hall of Aluminum Fame 75
Kal Kan 75
Ken-L Ration 75
kennel 24
kitchen accessories 55
Kmart 25

L

landscaping 15, 63
language 17
lanyard 50
Lassie 66
Leonida's Restaurant 75
lessons 40
licensing 30
line-cut passes 62
Lion King Celebration 42
long lines 45–46
lunch 31

M

Mad Hatter 62
Mad Hatter hats 58
magic moments 22–23
magic tricks 55
manage by example 12, 82
MasterCard 25
McDonald's 77
Mickey Mouse 13
Mickey Mouse Club 73
Mickey Mouse ears 57
Mickey's Gourmet Cookbook 53
Monorail 66
Monsanto Hall of Chemistry 75
Mr. Toad's Wild Ride 68
Muppet Vision 43
music 15

N

napkins 55
NBC 73
never finished 33
notepads 30

O

Ouimet, Matt 12

P

park-hopper 27
passport 26, 27
pencils 30, 55
pens 30
PeopleMover 74, 75
Pepsi-Cola 74, 75
personal touch 40
photographs 31
pin trader 49
pin trading 50–52
pins 30, 59
Pirates of the Caribbean 68, 74
plates 55
Platinum Card 80
Platinum Club 79
plush toys 30
popcorn 31, 59
postcards 31
Potter, Joe 74
Power of Story 41
pre-show 43–44
premium annual passport 28–29
Primeval World 74
Purina 75
purses 30

R

radio 49
readmission passes 62
recruiting 81
Refreshment Corner 76
rescue 49
restaurants 31
restaurants, leased 68, 74
Richfield 75
Rin Tin Tin 66
River Belle 83

Rocket to the Moon 75

S

sandwich makers 55
Santa Fe & Disneyland Railroad 75
service standards 21
service theme 20
silhouettes 59
Sklar, Marty 78
smile 12
Snow White's Scary Adventure 68
Soap Opera event 84
Soarin' Over California 43
soft drinks 31, 59
souvenir guides 37
souvenirs 31
Splash Mountain 41–42, 64
Star Tours 43, 64
Star Traders 64
strollers 31
Sunkist Citrus House 75
Sunkist I Presume 75
sweatshirts 30, 55
Swift's Red Wagon Inn 75

T

t-shirts 30, 55
television advertising 70
temporary duty assignment 84
Thomas, Carole Copeland 77
Titanium Card 80
Tool Time 30
tours 39–40
Town Square 62
toys 55
Traditions 17
trash can 47–48
trash, pick up 12, 48, 81
turkey legs 59
TWA 75

U

Upjohn Pharmacy 75

V

values 16–19
Visa 25

W

waffle irons 55
Walk with Walt tour 39, 79
walkie-talkies 31
WalMart 25
Walt Disney Travel Company 50
watches 30, 55
websites 70
Weiss, Al 12
wheelchairs 31
Wrather Corporation 66, 74
Wrather, Jack 66
Wurlitzer Music Hall 75

Y

Yale & Towne Lock Shop

About the Author

Rich Hamilton writes and speaks on customer service, selling, leadership, and business strategy. A former broadcast executive and newspaper reporter, Rich also has experience as a professional photographer and systems analyst. He has trained uncountable salespeople and helped many businesses with their marketing strategies.

Today, Rich consults and speaks on management skills that help create a sales-oriented company culture.

He has a special passion for the Disney business model, and has been studying it since 1986.

Rich Hamilton is available for a limited number of speaking engagements each year.

Richard Hamilton Associates offers behavior and values profiles for staff selection and management; learning systems for sales, marketing, and advertising; and consulting services.

Contact Information:

Richard Hamilton Associates
Phone: 602.438.2345 1.800.816.7710
Internet: www.SellBetter.com
Email: info@MagicStrategy.com
Mail Care of: SellBetter, Box 50186, Phoenix, AZ 85076

The Magic Moment Recognition Package

We've put together a special package for managers who want to implement a recognition program combining elements similar to Walt Disney World's Guest Service Fanatic card program and the Applause-O-Gram program. The Magic Moment Starter Pack Includes:

- 5,000 full-color pocket-size Major Magic Moment cards.
- 150 full-color Applause-O-Gram Recognition Certificates.
- 6 copies of *Disney Magic-Business Strategy* book.
- 1 copy of *Disney Magic-Business Strategy* audio cassette program.
- The Special *Magic Moment Recognition Program Manual* to use in implementation of the program, including checklists, a special audio cassette program describing how the programs work and how to coordinate them in various sizes of companies, and information about special recognition pins and periodic celebration meetings.

How to Get Other Products

Order additional copies of this book or our other products from the web site, by mail or by phone:

www.MagicStrategy.com
SellBetter Tools, Box 50186, Phoenix, AZ 85076
Tel. 800.434.1291

Disney Magic-Business Strategy book, ISBN 097284760X, 20.00
Internet Business Magic, ISBN 0972847618, 20.00
Disney Magic Ideabook, ISBN 0972847626, 20.00
Disney Magic-Business Strategy audio cassettes, 89.00
Disney Magic-Business Strategy audio CDs, 99.00
Magic Moment Recognition Plan Starter Pack, 997.00

Products with ISBN numbers may be purchased at better bookstores. Check website or phone for current pricing and additional products.

SellBetter™

Disney Magic Ideabook
Quick Order Form

Fax Orders: 1-800-819-9087. Send this form.
Telephone Orders: Call 1-800-434-1291 toll free. Have your credit card ready.
Email Orders: orders@SellBetter.com
Postal Orders: SellBetter Tools, PO Box 50186, Phoenix, AZ 85076 USA.

Please send the following books, disks, or reports. I understand that I may return any of them within 90 days for a full refund of the purchase price for any reason, no question asked.

_____

_____

_____

Please send more FREE information on:

   Other books   Speaking/Seminars   Consulting

Name:_____

Address:_____

City:_____ State_____ Zip_____-_____

Telephone:_____ Fax:_____

Email Address:_____

Sales Tax: Please add 8.1% for products shipped to Arizona addresses.*

Shipping and Handling:
US: $4 for the first book or disk and $2 for each additional product.
International: $9 for first book or disk; $5 for each additional product (estimate).

Payment: Check   Credit Card:
  American Express   Optima   Visa   MasterCard

Card Number_____

Name on card_____ Exp date:_____/_____
(Credit card orders must ship to credit card billing address.)

*Sales tax and prices subject to adjustment to current rates.

SellBetter™

Disney Magic Ideabook
Quick Order Form

Fax Orders: 1-800-819-9087. Send this form.
Telephone Orders: Call 1-800-434-1291 toll free. Have your credit card ready.
Email Orders: orders@SellBetter.com
Postal Orders: SellBetter Tools, PO Box 50186, Phoenix, AZ 85076 USA.

Please send the following books, disks, or reports. I understand that I may return any of them within 90 days for a full refund of the purchase price for any reason, no question asked.

_____

_____

_____

Please send more FREE information on:

    Other books   Speaking/Seminars   Consulting

Name:_____

Address:_____

City:_____State_____Zip_____-____

Telephone:_____Fax:_____

Email Address:_____

Sales Tax: Please add 8.1% for products shipped to Arizona addresses.*

Shipping and Handling:
US: $4 for the first book or disk and $2 for each additional product.
International: $9 for first book or disk; $5 for each additional product (estimate).

Payment: Check   Credit Card:
   American Express   Optima   Visa   MasterCard

Card Number_____

Name on card_____ Exp date:_____/_____
(Credit card orders must ship to credit card billing address.)

*Sales tax and prices subject to adjustment to current rates.

SellBetter™

Disney Magic Ideabook
Quick Order Form

Fax Orders: 1-800-819-9087. Send this form.
Telephone Orders: Call 1-800-434-1291 toll free. Have your credit card ready.
Email Orders: orders@SellBetter.com
Postal Orders: SellBetter Tools, PO Box 50186, Phoenix, AZ 85076 USA.

Please send the following books, disks, or reports. I understand that I may return any of them within 90 days for a full refund of the purchase price for any reason, no question asked.

_____

_____

_____

Please send more FREE information on:

    Other books   Speaking/Seminars   Consulting

Name:_____

Address:_____

City:_____ State_____ Zip_____-_____

Telephone:_____ Fax:_____

Email Address:_____

Sales Tax: Please add 8.1% for products shipped to Arizona addresses.*

Shipping and Handling:
US: $4 for the first book or disk and $2 for each additional product.
International: $9 for first book or disk; $5 for each additional product (estimate).

Payment: Check Credit Card:
   American Express Optima Visa MasterCard

Card Number_____

Name on card_____ Exp date:_____/_____
(Credit card orders must ship to credit card billing address.)

*Sales tax and prices subject to adjustment to current rates.